Emerging Technologies f

A Guide to Earning Money

Rajamanickam Antonimuthu

Introduction

This is Rajamanickam Antonimuthu. In this Book, I will discuss the significance of understanding emerging technologies and the numerous opportunities they offer. I also share my personal experiences of making money online, specifically through managing a YouTube channel.

The need to focus on Emerging Technologies

I used to wonder why I was able to earn money from my YouTube channel (YouTube.com/@QPT) with ease, compared to my other endeavors such as software development and website creation. I came to understand that the reason was related to my difficulties in building and retaining a strong software development team. Companies with established software development businesses could easily attract our skilled developers by offering higher salaries. However, when these companies first started, they didn't face such challenges as they were at the beginning of the software development era and thus, it was easier for them to succeed. Similarly, I received the benefits of starting a YouTube channel in the early days of the YouTube era, i.e., in 2009 itself..

With the advancement of computing power, increased network bandwidth, and widespread availability of mobile phones, people now prefer to consume content through videos rather than reading. This fast-paced growth of video production and consumption will change the entire business system.

For instance, people used to attend training centers to learn a new language or computer programming. Now, they can easily learn through tutorial videos on YouTube, causing a decline in training center businesses. To stay relevant, these businesses need to adapt and plan to offer their services through video platforms like YouTube.
While YouTube offers a great opportunity for earning money, it is also highly competitive. Many people have already started their own

YouTube channels on various topics, making it difficult to gain views. Additionally, YouTube is implementing new restrictions to enable monetization for new channels.

My experience highlights the importance of entering new business opportunities early on, as it is easier to make money. My story echoes the universal truth: the early bird gets the worm, especially when it comes to emerging technologies. My YouTube success hinged on being there at the dawn of video dominance. So, where are the next gold rushes? Look beyond YouTube—to the horizon where 3D printers churn out customized gadgets, robots dance in factories, and drones deliver your groceries. Buckle up for graphene revolutionizing materials, nanotech manipulating atoms, and AI assistants predicting your every move. Gene editing will rewrite the script of life, and desalination plants will quench our thirst. Buckle up for virtual worlds so real you'll need a vacation from reality, and wearables that track your every breath (and maybe even your thoughts). New batteries will power our world without wires, and driverless cars will take the wheel while we nap. Solar power will bathe us in clean energy, and quantum computers will crack the universe's secrets. And finally, imagine a future where your brain talks directly to your computer—no keyboard needed.

These are not science fiction fantasies; they're the building blocks of tomorrow. The time to learn, invest, and adapt is now. Don't be the software developer left behind by the YouTube boom. Be the visionary riding the wave of the next big thing. The future is calling, are you listening?

Some random thoughts about Emerging Technologies

While venturing into emerging technologies offers numerous benefits, it's crucial to remember not all will reach mainstream adoption. Therefore, navigating the world of upcoming technologies requires cautious investment of time and resources. While staying informed about emerging trends is vital, pouring all your money and dedicating all your time to a single technology can be risky..

Though research are happening on various emerging technologies, there is no guarantee for bringing them all into our everyday life in the near future. Some can be successful, some research may take more time, and some may never enter into our life. Just because a technology has been successfully researched doesn't mean it will be part of our daily life. Other related technologies also have to be successful for it to be useful. For example, AI algorithms were created many years ago, but they weren't useful at the time because we didn't have enough computing power. It wasn't until computing power grew that we started seeing AI being used in various fields.

Now we can see a lot of AI applications, e.g, discovering Drug, counting elephants, generating 3D holograms in real-time, detecting powdery mildew easily, analyzing satellite images, thought-to-speech system, improving the prediction of stroke recovery, fighting disinformation, teaching robots to make appropriate reactive human facial expressions, Diagnose Skin Conditions, Driverless Ride-Hailing Services, pinpoint Local Pollution Hotspots, explore the biomolecular world, Telehealth, speed up drug development, improving vaccine delivery, and many other things. You can check them at my YouTube channel.

Though we already started getting the benefits of AI, still various AI-related research are going on. For example, researchers are trying hard to develop Generic AI which can be used in any field. Personally, I witnessed the power of AI while running my YouTube channel. Previously I used to spend a lot of time and effort for creating subtitles/captions for my videos. Now, it can be done very easily without spending any time or effort. It is possible because of the AI which is improved a lot to understand anyone's voice and transcribe it automatically.

OpenAI's AI Tool ChatGPT can be used for writing articles, having discussions, writing stories, writing software code, writing tweets or promo texts for any social media, and even writing scripts for videos. Google also providing Bard to write article and software code.

People are afraid that AI will grab the job opportunities of them. Though it may not happen overnight, surely AI will affect the job market heavily in the long run. That's why Governments are working on Universal Basic Income schemes.

The wonder material Graphene is having a lot of potential to change our life entirely in the near future as it is having many unbelievable properties. Graphene is much harder than either steel or diamond of the same dimensions. It is the thinnest material possible as well as being transparent. It is completely impermeable. Even helium atoms can't pass through it.

Though we are seeing many kinds of applications (e.g protection of artworks, Bacteria-killing Shirts, Ultra-high-density hard drives, carbon capture, reducing paper industry energy costs, Graphene Microchip, heat pipes, memory resistors, anti-bacterial graphene face masks, smart textiles, light sail, Paint, Sieve turning Seawater into Drinking water, Thinnest Light Bulb) using Graphene, it is not yet commercialized in large scale.

Though we can simply create Graphene from Graphite found in pencils, by simply using sticking tape in the Lab in small amounts, it is still a challenge to produce pure graphene at a large scale. Researchers are working on producing graphene from plastics and tires. Some companies have started commercializing the Graphene applications like Fire pit and concrete slab.

Apart from large-scale production challenges, widespread Graphene usage is facing another issue also. People are afraid that Graphene will affect our health. For example, a few months back Canada banned Graphene Face Masks by citing Health risks as the reason.

Because of the huge developments happening in Artificial Intelligence and Material Science fields, many new inventions related to Robots and Drones are achieved. See them here. Most researchers are working on developing soft robots based on the inspiration from insects and animals, even they work on creating Living Robots.

I am noticing that scientists are trying to blur the difference between humans and robots by giving Humans the power of robots and by giving Human features to the Robots. Scientists built a Bionic Eye with better vision than humans. And, they are creating bionic "heart", bionic skin, Ocumetics Bionic Lens, Prosthetic Foot, and Inflatable robotic hand.

Brain-Computer Interfaces (BCI) are further helping to reduce the gap between Human and Robots. BCI allows Fast, Accurate Typing by people with Paralysis, and it enables paralyzed man to walk. It could control a Wheelchair, Vehicle, or Computer.

3D printing and Bioprinting technologies are making heavy impact on various fields including construction and medical. Researchers are working on to 3D print Concrete Houses, Human Corneas, Food, Stethoscope, Bricks, Ears, heart valve models, Glass, Hair, concrete bridge, Blood vessels, Smart Gel, and mini-liver. Researchers are working on 4D printing also.

Scientists are working on creating materials for neuromorphic computers which can operate similarly to Brains. And, they work on various things for Quantum Computers.

Gene-Editing Tools like CRISPR are playing important role in medical field. They could alleviate Depression, reverse retinitis pigmentosa, cure Cancer, create Low-Fat Pigs, lower Cholesterol, and enhance brain.

The combined power of AI, Nanotechnology, Quantum Computers, 3D printing, blockchain, and Gene-editing can help us to improve our life in the coming days.
But we need to note that we are facing many threats like climate change in the coming days. World's lakes losing oxygen rapidly as the planet warms. The Sahara Desert is Expanding. So, researches for fighting climate change may get more importance in the coming

days. Carbon capture related researches already started.

Ways to generate income from Emerging Technologies

Understanding emerging technologies offers two key benefits: increased personal convenience and enhanced professional opportunities.

There are several ways to earn money from emerging technologies, depending on your interests and skills. Here are a few ideas:

Investing: One way to earn money from emerging technologies is by investing in companies that are developing and commercializing these technologies. This could include investing in publicly traded tech companies or venture capital funds that specialize in early-stage startups. While emerging technologies can offer significant rewards, they also come with considerable risks. To navigate this landscape, diversify your investments and approach them with caution.

Consulting: If you have expertise in a specific area of emerging technologies, such as AI, blockchain, or cybersecurity, you could offer your services as a consultant to businesses and organizations that are looking to integrate these technologies into their operations.

Developing Apps or Software: If you have programming or software development skills, you could create your own apps or software that leverage emerging technologies, such as AR or IoT, and sell them to consumers or businesses.

Teaching or Training: As emerging technologies continue to reshape industries and job roles, there is increasing demand for professionals who have the skills and knowledge to work with these technologies. You could leverage your expertise to teach or train others, either through online courses or in-person workshops.

Writing or Speaking: If you have a talent for writing or public speaking, you could create content that educates others about emerging technologies, such as writing articles or blog posts, or speaking at industry conferences and events.

Creating and Selling Digital Products: If you have skills in graphic design, digital marketing, or content creation, you could create and sell digital products related to emerging technologies. This could include e-books, online courses, digital marketing materials, or templates for creating websites or mobile apps.

Developing Hardware Products: Emerging technologies often require specialized hardware components, and there is increasing demand for engineers and designers who can create and manufacture these components. If you have a background in hardware engineering or product design, you could develop and sell hardware products that leverage emerging technologies, such as smart home devices or wearable tech.

Offering Technical Support: As more businesses and consumers adopt emerging technologies, there is increasing demand for technical support services to help users troubleshoot issues and optimize their usage. If you have technical expertise in a specific area of emerging technologies, such as cloud computing or blockchain, you could offer your services as a technical support specialist.

Providing Data Analytics Services: Emerging technologies generate vast amounts of data, and there is increasing demand for professionals who can collect, analyze, and interpret this data to help businesses make informed decisions. If you have a background in data science or analytics, you could offer your services as a data analyst or consultant.

Developing Intellectual Property: As emerging technologies continue to evolve and mature, there is increasing demand for patents, trademarks, and other forms of intellectual property protection. If you have expertise in a specific area of emerging technologies, you could develop and patent new innovations, or help businesses and individuals navigate the intellectual property landscape.

Developing and Selling Digital Assets: As the use of emerging technologies expands, there is growing demand for digital assets such as cryptocurrency, non-fungible tokens (NFTs), and other blockchain-based assets. If you have experience in this area, you could develop and sell digital assets or offer services related to managing or investing in these assets.

Providing Security and Privacy Services: As more businesses and individuals use emerging technologies, there is increasing concern about security and privacy risks. If you have expertise in cybersecurity or privacy, you could offer your services to businesses and individuals to help them protect their digital assets and personal information.

Creating and Selling Educational Content: Emerging technologies are constantly evolving, and there is growing demand for educational content that helps people stay up-to-date with the latest trends and developments. If you have expertise in a specific area of emerging technologies, you could create and sell educational content such as online courses, e-books, or video tutorials.

Offering Design Services: As emerging technologies become more integrated into our daily lives, there is increasing demand for designers who can create interfaces and experiences that are user-friendly and visually appealing. If you have experience in design, you could offer your services to businesses and individuals looking to create products or experiences that leverage emerging technologies.

Providing Technical Writing Services: As emerging technologies become more complex and specialized, there is growing demand for technical writers who can create documentation and user manuals that are clear, concise, and easy to understand. If you have experience in technical writing, you could offer your services to businesses and individuals in need of documentation for their emerging technology products.

Offering Social Media Management Services: Social media platforms are an important way for businesses to reach customers and promote their products, and there is growing demand for social media managers who can create and execute effective social media strategies. If you have experience in social media marketing and management, you could offer your services to businesses looking to promote their emerging technology products.

Providing Virtual Reality (VR) or Augmented Reality (AR) Services: VR and AR are rapidly growing fields that are being used in a variety of industries, including gaming, education, and healthcare. If you have experience in VR or AR development, you could offer your services to businesses and organizations looking to create immersive experiences for their customers or users.

Developing Chatbots or Virtual Assistants: Chatbots and virtual assistants are becoming increasingly popular in industries such as customer service and e-commerce, and there is growing demand for developers who can create and deploy these tools. If you have experience in natural language processing or chatbot development, you could create and sell chatbots or offer your services to businesses looking to develop their own chatbots or virtual assistants.

Offering Blockchain Development Services: Blockchain technology is being used in a variety of industries, including finance, healthcare, and supply chain management. If you have experience in blockchain development, you could offer your services to businesses looking to develop blockchain-based products or services.

Providing AI or Machine Learning Services: AI and machine learning are being used in a variety of applications, including natural language processing, image recognition, and predictive analytics. If you have experience in AI or machine learning development, you could offer your services to businesses and organizations looking to develop AI-powered products or services.

Of course, these are just a few examples, and there are many other ways to earn money from emerging technologies depending on your background and interests. It's important to stay up-to-date with the latest trends and developments in this rapidly evolving field, and to identify opportunities to leverage your skills and expertise to create value for others.

Stay Ahead in Tech: Tips for Future-Proofing

It is not the strongest of the species that survives, nor the most intelligent that survives. It is the one that is most adaptable to change. - Darwin / Megginson

To keep up with the fast-paced world of technology, it's important to stay informed, learn new skills, embrace digital tools, and continually improve. By doing so, you'll be well-prepared for the future and ready to face any new technologies that come your way.

Here are some tips to help you prepare for the future of technology:

1. Stay informed: Read articles, follow experts, and attend events related to technology to keep up with the latest developments.
2. Learn new skills: Stay current with new technologies and trends by learning new skills and expanding your knowledge.
3. Network with peers: Attend industry events and meetups to connect with other professionals in your field.
4. Adopt a growth mindset: Be open to new ideas and be willing to adapt and change as technology evolves.
5. Embrace digital tools: Use technology to improve your work and increase your productivity.
6. Collaborate with others: Work with others in your industry to share knowledge and find solutions to challenges.
7. Stay curious: Ask questions, seek feedback, and challenge yourself to think critically about technology and its impact on society.
8. Focus on continuous improvement: Regularly assess your skills and knowledge, and make a plan to improve in areas where you need to grow.

By staying informed, learning new skills, and embracing new technologies, you can be well-prepared for the future of technology.

Here are some technology fields that are likely to play a significant role in career improvement in the coming days:

- Artificial Intelligence (AI) and Machine Learning (ML). Artificial Intelligence will become more advanced and will play a bigger role in our lives, from automating tasks to powering decision-making processes.
- Cloud Computing and Data Management
- Cybersecurity
- Internet of Things (IoT)
- Virtual and Augmented Reality. Virtual and Augmented Reality will become more immersive and will transform the way we work, play, and communicate.
- 5G Technology. The widespread adoption of 5G networks and the Internet of Things (IoT) will bring about faster, more reliable connectivity and a more connected world.
- Robotics and Automation
- Blockchain
- Natural Language Processing (NLP)
- Digital Marketing and Analytics

By acquiring skills in these technologies, professionals can remain competitive and enhance their career opportunities in the future. However, it's also important to continually evaluate new developments and stay adaptable to changes in the technology landscape.

Emerging technologies such as artificial intelligence, blockchain, cloud computing, and the Internet of Things, offer a wide range of business opportunities for entrepreneurs and companies. Some potential business opportunities in emerging technologies include:

- AI-powered products and services: Developing and selling AI-powered products and services such as virtual assistants, chatbots, or predictive analytics

tools can be a lucrative business opportunity.
- Blockchain applications: Building blockchain-based solutions for various industries, such as finance, healthcare, or supply chain management, can open up new business opportunities.
- Cloud computing services: Providing cloud computing services, such as infrastructure as a service, platform as a service, or software as a service, can be a profitable business model.
- IoT-based products and services: Developing and selling Internet of Things (IoT) products and services such as smart home devices, wearable technology, or industrial IoT solutions can be a promising business opportunity.
- Cybersecurity solutions: With the increasing number of cyber threats, there is a growing demand for cybersecurity solutions. Entrepreneurs can start a business in this field by offering security services such as network security, threat detection, or data protection.

These are just a few examples of the many business opportunities that exist in the emerging technologies. With the right combination of skills, resources, and market knowledge, entrepreneurs and companies can take advantage of these opportunities and succeed in the fast-paced world of technology.

Jobs and businesses that are heavily reliant on manual or repetitive tasks, as well as those that can be easily automated, are at risk of becoming obsolete in the near future. This includes jobs in industries such as manufacturing, data entry, and telemarketing. On the other hand, jobs and businesses that require creative thinking, emotional intelligence, and critical problem-solving skills are less likely to become obsolete. These include careers in fields such as education, healthcare, and technology. However, with the rapid pace of technological advancement, it is important for workers and entrepreneurs to continuously acquire new skills and adapt to changing market demands.

In conclusion, it's imperative to be aware of emerging technologies to keep your job and business relevant in the ever-evolving job market. With automation and new technologies changing the job market rapidly, it's important to continuously acquire new skills and adapt to the changing market demands. By staying informed and embracing new technologies, you can increase your chances of staying competitive in the job market and securing a promising future for your career or business. Don't let technological advancements leave you behind; be proactive and stay ahead of the curve.

My Tips for doing online business

Find below my general suggestions for people interested in starting online businesses. These suggestions are applicable for any kind of business including businesses related to emerging technologies.

- Make sure that your Product/service actually helps to solve people's problems. It should be either entertaining or educational.

- Don't spend much in the initial stage. Do the scaling only after testing the market with a simple version of your product. This particularly important for any products involving emerging technologies.

- Don't try to copy successful businesses. Instead, build your business based on your own skills, and market situations at the time of starting your business. Starting a business related to emerging technologies will be easy and the success rate will be high. So, always learn about emerging technologies and make sure that you are not misguided by any false promises as no one can predict the future of emerging technologies.

- Don't be greedy. If you are greedy, mostly you will be cheated by scammers.

- You need to understand the fact that succeeding in online business is not easy. You need to put in a lot of effort and withstand a lot of failures. You need a lot of courage to withstand failures and re-start with the same enthusiasm after fixing what made you fail.

- You should understand that starting an online business is very easy. For example, a complete e-commerce site can be set up in a few hours without spending much. But things like doing proper testing, promotion/marketing, customer support, and maintenance of the site require a lot of effort and spending.

- Give more importance to hiring a great Team. If you couldn't find great Team members, it is better not to hire anyone instead of hiring some average or low-performing candidate.

Let me share some details about how to start an online business. I am writing it in a very general way. Doing actual business will vary based on various factors, like your skill set, competition, resources, regulations, compliances, etc.

Once you decide to start an online business, you need to decide your product or service. Select your product/service based on your own interest and skill. If you are interested in music, you can sell your own albums or just run a youtube channel from which you can earn money from ads, sponsors, merch, membership, affiliates, etc.

Having your own website will be an advantage for doing online business, though you can do online business through other social media websites or by using free blogging sites. Owning a website won't cost much. You need to register a domain with domain providers like Godaddy and you need to have a hosting to keep files of your website. Generally, Godaddy itself will sell hosting services. But I heard that generally domain providers are not good at hosting.

So, it is better to have a hosting service from a company that is good at hosting. I use HostGator for many years without any issues. We can easily point the domain from the domain provider to our website at the hosting provider by doing a simple DNS entry.

We need to be very careful in choosing the domain name. It should reflect our brand name, and it should be easy to remember, it shouldn't create any confusion, and it should not violate anyone's trademark.

Another important thing is the pricing of the domain name. Though the domain names won't cost much, you need to remember that we should renew them every year. Most domain providers provide huge discounts initially, but we need to pay higher prices without discounts when renewing them. So, keep this in mind when deciding to have your own website. If you are on a tight budget, you may simply start using free blogging services. In this case, you need not pay for domain and hosting, everything will be free. Actually, my main blog (blog.qualitypointtech.com) is hosted with Blogger which is free and allowed me to link my own domain.

While choosing a hosting service, they may offer various plans. Choose the plan which is more suitable for your requirements. It is better to start with a low-price plan, then we can move on to higher plans based on the necessity.

Once after buying a domain name and hosting, you can start developing your website for doing online business. One important thing is, you need to be very clear about your target audiences. It is very important from various perspectives. Even for choosing a hosting service, your target audience is important. If your target audiences are in the US and you host your website in India, the website will be loading slowly for your US audiences even though it loads quickly in India. In case, you are planning to target a global audience, it is better to use CDN services like Cloudflare which is having free options also. Apart from helping to load your site quickly throughout the world, the CDNs will provide a lot of security features and performance improvement services.

We need to be very tough in keeping our websites free from hacking attacks and spammers, otherwise, our entire efforts in doing business will be spoiled.

For developing a website, I would recommend WordPress which is free, open-source, and supported by almost all of the hosting services. It is very very easy to set up a WordPress site. Maintenance and customization are also easy. We can expand the functionality of the site by adding the required plugins. A lot of free plugins are available. For example, we can set up a complete e-commerce website within a few minutes with a lot of useful features without spending any money. We have to set the plugins for handling cache to reduce the server load and improve page serving speed, set up security-related plugins, set up plugins to add analytics code, etc. But we shouldn't add unnecessary plugins.

Starting a website is easy, but bringing potential customers to the website is the real challenge. We need to do digital marketing effectively and do lead capture and follow-ups properly.

And, we need to make sure that our website is loading quickly. It should appear correctly on various devices like Desktop computers, Tablets, Mobile phones, etc. There are various free tools available to check the page loading performance and checking mobile-friendliness.

Once you are ready with your products and your website developed to sell your products, you can not expect sales immediately even though you bring your potential customers to your sites through campaigns. Because no one is going to buy from a random person. You need to have social proof or you have to establish your brand name. You can achieve it in various ways. For example, if you are selling your ebook, you first start selling through Amazon. Once after getting significant reviews and ratings you can start selling through your own website. Similarly, if you are planning to work on freelancing projects, you can first work through freelance websites till establishing a good reputation. After that, you can sell your freelancing service through your website itself.

One important approach for getting a reputation/branding is writing a lot of good quality and useful articles on your blog. Write articles related to your products and share them through various social media sites consistently, especially write about your personal experiences related to your products, how you are developing your products, and the story behind choosing those products. Encourage people to subscribe to your free newsletter and send your articles through the newsletter. Once people are familiar with you, you can start telling them about your services or product sales through the newsletter. i-e you need to follow the proper funneling, starting from content marketing. And lead capturing is also important. People who are going through your product details may not buy it immediately. They may take some time to analyze your product and compare the price/quality/shipping/payment methods with your competitors. You have to do the lead-capturing properly to follow up with them later by offering discounts to make the sales. Lead-capturing can be done by various methods. For example, if you are selling computers, you get the email id for sending free ebooks about various computers, their maintenance, links to download the best free software for the computers, and best practices of using computers and troubleshooting them.

Once you are ready with your products and website built with key things, like good performance, easy navigation, proper lead-capturing system, and customer support system, you can start promoting through various ways, like, SEO, Social media promotion, PPC campaigns, email campaigns, affiliate marketing, running PPC campaigns, etc.

Doing SEO and running PPC campaigns is very important. I used to talk about these things in detail in my YouTube Live sessions. In the case of SEO, we need to focus on both on-page optimization and off-page optimization. Traffic from Search engines like Google is highly targeted traffic, so the sales conversion rate will be good. It is free and continuous traffic. But these days, it is difficult to rank high on search engines because of heavy competition. So, we need to consider spending money on doing PPC campaigns also. And, by doing our business related to emerging technologies, we will be able to able rank well for our keywords because of the low competition in the emerging technologies. That's why we need to do business related to emerging technologies.

Imagining the Future

Predicting our future world has become increasingly challenging due to the rapid evolution of new technologies. Just a few decades ago, we could not have imagined the extent to which our lives would be influenced by the internet and related technologies today. Many experts believe that the fourth industrial revolution will introduce even more transformative technologies that will greatly impact our lives in the coming years. Therefore, it has become very difficult to envision what our future world will look like.

Let's consider some possible scenarios. The rapid advancements in computing power, artificial intelligence, quantum computing, IoT, and material science are expected to drive widespread automation across various fields. This could enhance productivity and safety while also affecting job opportunities for humans. Initially, this may seem like a negative development, but in reality, people can receive financial support through Universal Basic Income schemes without having to work. Several countries have already conducted pilot studies on the implementation of Universal Basic Income, and the results have been encouraging. Contrary to popular belief, this approach has motivated people to pursue their interests rather than becoming lazy due to the availability of money without work. This ultimately leads to an improvement in overall productivity.

Developments of nanodevices will improve the medical field by improving drug delivery, imaging, monitoring, etc. Tiny cameras can be swallowed as pills to diagnose diseases. Once CRISPR Gene editing comes into the mainstream, the entire medical field will see a major change. We will be able to cure a lot of diseases easily, apart from creating designer babies. And, people started talking about artificial womb which can help to avoid pregnancy burdens. The advancements in developing Bionic devices are blurring the differences between humans and machines. Overall the medical field is trying to improve our health and increase our lifetime. But it will create an issue also. i-e It will create a society filled with many aged people. It creates the need for social robots for helping the elderly.

While we see improvements in our lifestyle and health, our Earth is facing climate change problems. Many scientists are saying that it will become a huge issue if we do not take the required actions as soon as possible. So, many research groups have already started developing carbon capture technologies. And drinking water issues are also becoming a big problem in many places. That's why scientists are exploring various desalination techniques to get drinking water from seawater.

Looking back at history, we can know the fact that our lives may be affected by technological changes in some way. But the core part of our lives is mostly independent of technology. We can always find happiness and peace in our lives by focusing on good things like love, courage, gratitude, and integrity while avoiding negative things like jealousy and greediness. This fundamental fact is not changing irrespective of time and technologies. Anyway, it is always good to keep an eye on emerging technologies to improve our careers in the coming days.

My experiences of Earning Money Online

Because of the widespread usage of the internet, traditional business models are getting changed entirely. These days we have a lot of opportunities for earning money online. I won't say that earning money online becomes easy, but the opportunities for earning money online are increasing, and we get a lot of information and guidance for earning money online.

As I sit down to write this, the world might not hold me up as a paragon of success (though, deep down, my own story sings a different tune). I get it. Most seek out the triumphant narratives, the gilded tales of those who have scaled the summit. But in our insatiable hunger for "how-to" guides, we often overlook a crucial factor: survivorship bias.

What is survivorship bias? It's the tendency to only see the successes, the ones who made it, neglecting the countless others who poured in equal, if not greater, effort but haven't yet reached their peak. It's like peering at a mountain range through a narrow lens, only seeing the triumphant peaks, oblivious to the valleys of struggle and the climbers still scaling their own paths.

Learning purely from the "made it" crowd can be limiting. Their stories, while inspiring, often gloss over the nitty-gritty, the stumbles, the near misses. It's the unsung heroes, the ones who persevere despite delayed gratification, who offer a richer tapestry of lessons. They share not just the triumphant "what" but also the crucial "how" – the detours, the pivots, the resilience forged in the face of setbacks.

That's why, despite not yet wielding the financial gold medal, I choose to share my journey in this chapter. It's not about proving anything to the world, but about offering a different perspective, a glimpse into the less-charted territories of the success landscape. My story might not be a shiny trophy on the shelf, but it's a weathered map, marked with both triumphs and tribulations, offering valuable insights for fellow travelers.

Moreover, my experiences highlight the need for doing any business related to emerging technologies.

So, buckle up, dear reader, for a ride beyond the usual success stories. We're venturing into the realm of the "almost there," the "still striving," the ones who refuse to let setbacks dim their inner fire. And who knows, maybe, just maybe, in the echoes of my own challenges and triumphs, you'll find the missing piece of your own unique path to success.

Before giving more details, I want to clarify a few things.

I am going to write this chapter based on my personal experiences. I haven't done any research to come up with this. I am just writing it based on my own experiences and my own thoughts. So, it need not be applicable to everyone.   In the case of online earnings, you may come across a lot of scams and misinformation. So, you need to be very careful about doing online works.

My Name is Rajamanickam Antonimuthu. I have completed my Engineering Degree in 1998 in India and had worked for various IT companies including IT wings of big investment banks such as BNY and CitiGroup in various roles (mostly in software test automation) till 2008.

Then I wanted to start doing my own Business.   I explored various business options. Since I had good work experiences in Software

Development and Software Testing, I decided to do freelance work related to Software Development or Testing.

Since I am living in a Developing Country, doing freelance work for a local market is not profitable. So, I started looking for online work. I thought doing freelance work online for the clients living in 'Developed Countries' can help me to earn significant money. I spent significant time at Browsing Centers (Net Cafe) for using the internet to search for online work. It was not easy to get online work at that time period. I was ready to do any kind of online work including Data Entry work. But I found difficulty in finding online work. I thought having an internet connection at my home can help me to spend more time searching for online work. But it was not easy to get an internet connection at that time. Somehow I managed to get an internet connection at my home, and started spending more time searching on the internet to find online work. Initially, I was not looking for any money, and I was ready to do any kind of task without any payment just to start my online career. But still, I was not able to get any online work for many weeks.

I put a lot of effort for finding freelance websites, as there were only a few freelance websites available at that time. And I started spending a lot of time for searching work on those freelance websites. After some weeks of continuous efforts, finally I got my first task from a freelance website called "RentACoder" which was later renamed to "vWorker" and then merged with "Freelancer". Interestingly, my first task was completely irrelevant to my skill set. It was related to video-editing which I was not familiar at that time. It was not an actual video-editing task, but a question related to video-editing. Somehow I managed to complete the task (i-e answering the question) by referring to many websites and doing a lot of Trail and Error actions, and I got a good rating and review comment. I felt very happy about it and decided to continue this approach.

Interestingly I was able to complete this first task within an Hour though I had to spend a lot of hours to get this project. Initially, I used to bid for a lot of projects. Then I realized that placing a lot of bids is not going to help even if my bids are very low. Instead of putting my efforts into bidding on a lot of projects, I started bidding on a few highly relevant projects and put my efforts into analyzing those projects deeply. I started asking a lot of relevant questions after going through the requirements, and even I started telling my suggestions for the success of the projects even before winning the bids. This approach helped me to win more bids and I put a lot of hard work to deliver the projects as per the requirements of the customers. I did the corrections without any hesitation. All these things helped me to get good ratings and bonus money.

I started getting exclusive projects so that I can win the bid without any competition. I focused more on PHP/MySQL projects.

As I was getting more projects easily, I started a Company "QualityPoint Technologies" and started hiring Team members to help me complete the projects. Because of the quality of our work and competitive bidding, we used to get many projects and we were able to complete more than 120 projects within a few years.

Though I had a lot of Good Ratings and Reviews for my RentACoder profile, my account got suspended for a dispute with a customer. By that time, I had a list of good customers who were willing to give me the projects directly. So the RentACoder account suspension didn't affect my business. Instead, it helped me to avoid their fees and I got the freedom to have direct communication with the clients without any restrictions. The only thing was I couldn't see the Reviews and Ratings given by the clients as my account got suspended. Interestingly, all these Reviews started appearing on my profile at Freelancer which acquired RentACoder. It made me think that no one can stop the rewards of our Hard work. Anyway, I didn't want to use any freelancing websites as I got enough projects from my existing customers. More interestingly, my blog post about the RentACoder account suspension got a lot of traffic, and I earned some money by adding an affiliate link to another freelance website.

In case you decide to use freelancing websites for your online earnings, first spend significant time for finding a freelancing site which is most suitable to you. Then understand their rules properly by going through the discussions on related forums. Once you are familiar with their rules, features, and best practices, spend significant time for properly setting up your profile or any other details like skill set, hourly rate, etc. As I specified earlier, try to understand the requirements of the project properly and come up with your questions when bidding for the project. As a beginner, you may have to bid low to get projects. But don't bid too low. Always have clear communication with your customer. Don't hesitate to point out any issues in their requirements. When you face any difficulty in completing the project at the specified time period, immediately communicate with your customer, don't give them surprises. It is better to get the payment on Hourly basis in the long run. Most of the customers may not agree to pay Hourly as they plan to spend a specific amount of money for a specific project. So, they prefer to pay based on the project rather than Hourly. But it is important to gain their trust to convince them for the Hourly payment. The main reason is, we tend to give our suggestions only when we are paid hourly. Our suggestions are very important for the success of the project. We will be getting more projects only when our customers are successful. It is better to focus on specific area of work. For example, if you are a coder, focus on any one specific script (e.g PHP). In the long run, you will be coming up with a lot of function libraries which you can reuse in many of the projects. It will help you to save time and get more projects easily.

Let me continue my story. Though I could get projects easily, I couldn't earn money as the employees used to leave our Company for a better salary from Corporate Companies once they got experience from our company. All my energy, time, and money spent on hiring the Team members and for training them were not helping me to earn money. So, I decided to change our business model. I focused more on developing and promoting our own products such as Timesheet Software. This business model is somewhat better than the previous one, because the high employee attrition rate didn't affect this model much. In the case of Freelance projects, we used to get different kinds of projects. So, it required good work experience in various kinds of projects. But in case of timesheet project, I can easily train any new team member.

But this model is also not giving much profit as the advertising cost is high.

In short, getting projects becomes easy for me. Individually I could earn from the projects. But it was not profitable when I tried to do it by hiring Team members. i-e I was not able to scale this business model.

In the meantime, I have noticed that Google Adsense is giving significant earnings from my blog which I started to share my software development experiences initially. So, I had decided to choose Google Adsense earnings as the primary source of income. And therefore, I have started many websites for showing Adsense ads.

I even sold many websites through websites-market-places such as Flippa and Digitalpoint Forum by showing the Adsense revenue as the proof for the value of the website. These things made me think that Google Adsense is the best and easy way of earning online. Anyway, flipping of websites didn't help much as I faced difficulty while selling many websites.

Sometimes the Fees for selling the website are more than the website sales price itself. And, the instability in our Team causes high development and promotion costs. Unnecessarily I was spending money for renewing many domains, and for the hosting servers. So, finally I decided to drop lots of websites by letting them expire themselves instead of wasting my time and money for trying to sell them through Flippa or any other websites-market place.

The unstable Team causes a lot of issues. For example, I have done a lot of hard work to bring the Automatic Resume Posting tool which had lots of potential to earn money easily. But, because of the instability in our Team, I couldn't make money from that amazing thing.

And therefore, I stopped hiring any new Team members to avoid further losses driven by unstable team.

Currently, I don't have any full-time team member. But I strongly believe in Team work. And, I had a lot of good experiences when we were working as a Team.   So, I have plans to build a Strong Team in the near future once I finalize my current business plans.

I learned the lesson that unstable Team won't allow the Entrepreneur to earn money from any kind of initiative even if all the other things are supporting the Entrepreneur.

I am exploring various ways about making the unstable Team into a stable team.

In the meantime, I had decided to find some other ways for earning money without depending on Team members much. i-e I was looking for some kind of passive income opportunity.

I had tried various ways for earning passive income including, website flipping, Affiliate Programs, publishing Books, Android Apps, etc,   But I feel YouTube is the best among all the tried ways.

I had spent lots of Time, Money, and Energy for trying all other things. But they haven't given any significant benefits. Surprisingly, I started earning significant money from my YouTube videos without spending any money for doing it.

And, I did some analysis about future trends, and found that YouTube is the one among the 3 important online businesses, while Mobile Apps and Social Media are the other two things. I thought running YouTube Channel is comparatively easy among these 3 things. So, I decided to focus more on YouTube.

Apart from earning money by showing Google Adsense Ads, you can earn money from YouTube Videos through many other different ways also. For example, YouTube allows you to sell Merchandise by adding the link to the products using YouTube Cards in your videos. YouTube is having list of Merchandise partners.

I had tried to sell the products like T-Shirts from Spreadshirt which is one of the YouTube Merchandise partners. It was not successful for me. Because my channel audiences are from many different Countries and I upload videos on different topics. So it didn't work for me.

For example audiences from India may not purchase these T-shirts as they can easily get these T-shirt at a very low price from their local shops. But it may work well for the YouTubers who focus on specific audience. Their success possibility will be very high if they found merchandise best suitable for their audience.

I came to know that YouTube's other Merch Partner Teespring is helping to earn money. So, now I have decided to explore it. I designed some T-Shirts and linked the Teesping account with my Youtube Account so that the T-Shirts will be automatically displayed under each of my youtube videos.

We can set our own price for our Merch products and we can promote it by giving Discount code also. I had tried this option for a few months. I had spent significant time and effort to create T-Shirt designs. I am not good at design. So, I tried creating simple designs with various Quotes and trending topic slogans. All these efforts were not much useful. I got a few sales only. So, I disabled this feature.

Before telling about YouTube further, let me first share my other earning experiences.

In my blog, I shared my software testing experiences in many blog posts. Those posts were viewed by a lot of people. So, I decided to combine all those posts and created as an eBook. I sold it from my website. It was selling well. So, I published it as a Kindle book on Amazon and then published a paperback version through Createspace. I earned significant money from the sales of this Book. But this book is bit outdated now. So, it is not selling now.

After seeing the success of this Book, I had published a few other books, but they were not successful. I spent significant money for running paid campaigns for promoting the Books. I tried Google Ads, Facebook Ads, Reddit ads, GoodReads Give-Away, LinkedIn Ads, Book Deals sites, and Amazon AMS ads. But they were not much helpful. But I am still exploring the option of book publishing as a way of earning money to handle the risk in case I face any unexpected issues with my YouTube earnings.

As explained earlier, I closed most of my websites started with the aim of earning money from Google AdSense. But I didn't want to close one site named TheQuotes.Net as I like this name much and I am partnered with my friend for running this website. As part of promoting this website, I had decided to develop an android App, and I came to know that I can earn money by showing admob ads. So, I learned to use Android Studio to develop simple Apps.

Though the Quotes app got a lot of good ratings, my earnings from this App is not much. But still, I published a few other Android Apps as a way of promoting my other products.

I am putting significant efforts for doing Amazon affiliate marketing. As of now, I am not seeing any significant growth there. But, I am continuing my efforts for doing it. Because YouTube disabled monetization for my YouTube Channel two times by saying duplicate content as reason. So, as a backup revenue stream, I am continuing Affiliate marketing though I am not earning from it as of now.

Let me share my YouTube experience now. I had created my YouTube Channel "QualityPointTech" (YouTube.com/@QPT) in the year 2009. Initially, I was not taking YouTube as a serious business option. At that time I was concentrating on doing software/web development business. Apart from doing software development, I was running a blog for sharing my knowledge and experience of doing Software Testing and Web development. And, I came to know about the fact that many people are earning money by showing Google Adsense ads in their blogs.

So, I thought of trying that option, and therefore I applied for Google Adsense. But my request got rejected many times. Finally, after many attempts, Google granted me Google Adsense, and I started showing Google Adsense ads in my blog. It took a few months to earn my first Google Adsense Cheque. During those days, Google used to send the Adsense payment as a Cheque once after our earning exceeds $100.

Within a few months, I started getting Google's Payment Cheque every month regularly. I realized the earning potential of my blog which was started just to showcase my software testing and development skills to get freelance projects. So, I decided to spend significant time in promoting the blog. For promoting our blog, I created my YouTube Channel. i-e That time I considered YouTube as one of the link submitting websites which can help to improve the search rank of my blog in Google Search.

A few months later, I received an email from YouTube saying that I have the opportunity to earn money from YouTube videos by linking   my Google Adsense account with my YouTube account. And, I added Google Adsense ads to my YouTube Videos. But I haven't focused much on creating YouTube videos. I just used it for promoting my blog and our Timesheet product. One day, one of my Videos about Google Doodle got significant views and thereby I earned significant money.

This incident had taught me about the fact of how YouTube Videos are behaving differently comparing with blogs. I came to know that YouTube Videos are getting more views for Trending Topics i-e topics that are searched by many users suddenly. Thereafter I switched my focus from doing web development to creating YouTube videos. I made this decision due to other reason also i-e Problems faced in Web development business due to the unstable Team as I explained earlier.

I continued uploading videos about Trending Topics regularly, and earning money from those videos. But I felt that it is not going to be a stable business model for long time. Because I strongly believe that any business which is not solving people's problems is not going to survive for long time. So, I explored various other things which can really solve People's problems or help them in some ways.

For example, I thought about adding Tutorial videos which can help people to learn software development and software testing.   But, I have noticed that a lot of other Channels were already providing Tutorial Videos. And, I found that there were   very few Channels only available for giving latest Science and Technology News. So, I have decided to use our YouTube channel for giving Science and Technology News.

Comparing to the Trending Topics Videos, the Technology News Videos are getting very less number of Views only. But I am spending a lot of Time and Effort for uploading Technology News Videos regularly. Because I came to know that many Scientists and Inventors are inventing many useful things, and they are publishing their findings in many Journals. But the benefits of their inventions are reaching the end-users after a very long time only. The reason for this unwanted delay is, the latest science and technology news is not reaching the Entrepreneurs who can bring it further to the end-users. I believe our YouTube Channel can fill this Gap. So, I will continue to upload Science/Technology News Videos even if they are not earning much.

Whenever I go through the YouTube Earning related questions in Quora, I see two types of Questions. One is, people asking about earning huge money from YouTube, that too quickly and easily. They are seeing YouTube as a magic money-making machine. I can clearly say that YouTube is NOT suitable for that kind of people. It may be true that many people are earning Millions of Dollars from YouTube just by uploading few videos that are just showing themselves playing Computer Games. But this is not going to work for everyone.

The another type of Quora Questions about YouTube is, people asking about earning money from YouTube by utilizing their specific skills, like, Music, Dance, Teaching, etc. YouTube will be best suitable for them, not only for earning Money, but for their Career improvements also.

For example, assume that you are a Musician. You can start your YouTube Channel easily and immediately without spending any Money. You have to upload your Music Videos to your Channel frequently. Many people will start watching your video. If people are watching your music videos long time, YouTube will start suggesting your video to many people. Because Watch Time of the Video is an important factor for YouTube to find whether a video is interesting or not. So, obviously your channel will get more views, and you will start earning money.

Apart from earning money you will get feedback and suggestions from your audience through the comments. Apart from making ad revenue, you can earn by selling your albums to your established audiences. And, note that just uploading video is not enough, you need to give meaningful and attractive Title, add relevant Tags and most importantly you should promote your Videos. i-e You need to share your video link with your friends and on social media like Facebook, Twitter, etc. And you may earn additional money by teaching Music to the people who are interested to learn from you. And, you need to report to YouTube if you find any other YouTube channel stealing your videos.

If you are not interested to spend time in promotion activities and preventing video stealing, you can join an MCN (Multi-Channel Network) so that they can take care of those things on behalf of you. But you should remember that not all the MCNs are good, some of them may be worst and fraud. I never used any MCN. So, do your research before joining any MCN.

The very first question from the people who are willing to make earnings from YouTube is like "How much money I will get for Thousand Views?" You need to understand that view count is not the appropriate measure for calculating revenue. Your YouTube earning will depend on various other factors also.

Based on my understanding, I feel my YouTube Earnings depend on below parameters. There may be many other parameters which I may not be knowing yet.

Video Topic. Normally technology videos earn more than entertainment videos.

Country of the viewers. If your audience are from U.S, U.K and Canada, you can earn more.

Length of the Video. Based on my observation, long videos tend to earn more money than short videos. (Note that long video means the duration of the part actually watched by the viewers)

Traffic Source. You can earn money more if the viewers are coming from Google search, instead of from any social media site.

Note that we can use our YouTube Channel for doing Live Streaming also. You can do it from your mobile devices too using YouTube App.

In Desktop you can use any broadcasting software like OBS for broadcasting   Live programs to your YouTube Channel. And, YouTube is providing features like "Super Chat" which will allow you to earn money by highlighting user chat comments while broadcasting your live video.

I learn lots of things from the feedback/comments given by my channel viewers. Many people told me that my voice/accent is not understandable for them. So, I am spending significant time in adding subtitle / CC for almost every video I upload. YouTube is providing a Tool for making the subtitle adding task easy. If you give the entire transcript of the video, it will automatically create the subtitle for your Video. Adding subtitle will help to increase the watch time of the video and therefore it will help to get more views.

And YouTube is providing an automatic translation option also. But I haven't used it much and therefore I can not tell about the impact of using automatic translation.

I did the mistake of not buying a good quality microphone. This mistake affected my channel growth heavily. I realized my mistake after a few years only, and bought a good quality Mic and Stand for holding the Mic.

So, make sure that you are using Good Quality Mic and Camera or any other tool required for creating your videos.

For improving Voice quality, I started using the audio tools like Audacity. I use it for doing noise removal and for removing silence.

I spent significant time creating custom Thumbnail image for my videos. Actually, YouTube will allow you to choose one of its 3 automatic thumbnail suggestions. But it will be better to create our own thumbnail image and upload it as a custom thumbnail.

For promoting our YouTube Videos, I follow many different ways. I share my videos on social media sites and I will specify my YouTube Video in my answers in any Q&A Website or Forums. I joined with many relevant Facebook Groups.

And, I have released a Mobile App in Google Play Store for viewing our YouTube Channel. I am embedding most of my videos in my news website Jone.Live so that people can easily navigate my YouTube Channel Videos based on Tags and Categories.

I used to spend significant time in going through YouTube Analytics which gives lots of information about our Videos, like Ad Rate, Watch time, Demographics, Traffic sources, details about Likes, Shares, Comments, Playlists etc. And, it provides Real Time stats also. We can get lots of clue from these Analytics Stats to improve our Channel. So, it is very important to go through YouTube Analytics regularly.

We need to be very careful while promoting our videos. We should promote our videos in genuine ways at relevant places only. If you promote your video to irrelevant audience, then the watch time of your video will be reduced. Good watch time is an important factor for earning from YouTube videos.

Another important thing you need to be very careful about is, Copyright Rules. Never violate anyone's Copyright and Privacy. Try to be familiar with YouTube's Terms & Conditions, Policies, Copyright rules and Community guidelines. You will get copyright strikes for violating anyone else's copyright. And you will get Strikes for violating the Community Guidelines also.

Note that your Strike will not go even if you delete the Video. Your YouTube account will be terminated if you get three strikes. You can not create any new account. So, be very careful about copyrights and community guidelines.

And never try to click the ads in your own videos. It may lead to your Adsense account termination.

Sometimes we may receive false copyright notices due to incorrect functioning of YouTube's ContentID matching system. So, you need to dispute those false claims, otherwise the ad revenue from your video will be paid to copyright claimer.

At sometimes, YouTube will allow you to remove the copyrighted song from your video instead of deleting the entire video. And, I have noticed that we will not be able to edit some details of a video if that video exceeds significant views.

Sometimes, I used to think about why I could earn from YouTube easily comparing with my other initiatives like Software Development and Web Sites. In fact I am NOT good at video creation. I realized that it is related to the fact about why I couldn't build strong software Development Team even when I was working very hard to achieve that mission. The Answer is simple. I couldn't compete with the already established software development companies in terms of retaining skilled developers.

Those companies easily attract our team members by offering higher salaries. But when they started their business a few decades back, they didn't face these problems. Because they were at the beginning of software development era. For them, it was easy to succeed in Software Development Business. I understand that I am experiencing the same thing with YouTube. i-e Succeeding in any Emerging Industry/Market is easy comparing to competing with already saturated industry. I believe Video is Emerging now. When Printers were invented, there was a business opportunity for putting all the knowledge and experience of humans in Books format.

Once Computers were invented, there was a demand for converting the Books into Digital format by doing Data Entry tasks. Then there was a demand for Web Developers for putting those digital data into websites so that people can access them from anywhere. Now people are preferring to consume those content simply by watching as video instead of reading the content by themselves.

The fast growth of computing power, increased network bandwidth and accessibility of Mobile Phones made their wish possible. And, this kind of fast growth of Video production and consumption is going to change the entire business systems.

For example, previously people used to join any Training Center for learning any new language or computer programming language. Now they can easily learn any new language by watching Tutorial videos on YouTube. So, the Training Center business will be going down, they need to slightly change their business model. They need to plan for doing their business through video platforms like YouTube.

It is true that YouTube is having a huge opportunity to earn money. But that doesn't mean that it is without competition.

Already a lot of people had started YouTube Channels on numerous Topics. Getting views to our YouTube channel is very difficult. Sometime back, I got a chance to meet many YouTube Video Creators at an Event arranged by YouTube. In the meeting, most of new video creators were saying that they found it very hard to earn money from their YouTube channels.

And, YouTube is also adding many new restrictions for enabling monetization for new channels. So, if you are planning to earn money from YouTube, you need to do it soon.

From my experience story, anyone can easily understand that entering earlier into any kind new business opportunities is the easy way of making money.

So, it is important to be familiar with the updates of Emerging Technologies such as 3D Printing, Robotics, Drones, Graphene, Nano Technology, Artificial Intelligence (AI)/Machine Learning, Gene Editing, Desalination Techniques, Virtual Reality, Wearables, New kinds of Batteries, Driver-less Cars, Solar Power Improvements, Quantum Computing, Brain–computer interface, etc.

I have uploaded a lot of Emerging Technologies-related videos to my YouTube channel, and daily I am spending a lot of time and effort to find the latest Science and Technology News from various sources including Universities, such as MIT, Stanford, Harvard and UC. And, I used to check various Science and Technology related groups in various social media websites to find latest updates of

Emerging technologies so that I can upload a news video about them. I would like to make my YouTube channel as a bridge connecting the Scientists and Business People.

While YouTube presents exciting opportunities, it also carries inherent risks. I, for instance, encountered issues like demonetization and Adsense account suspension, despite diligently adhering to their terms and conditions.

I believe Emerging Technologies will change our Life and Businesses entirely very soon.

So, if you are interested to know the latest technology news, subscribe to my YouTube channel.

As of now, I am not an expert in any kind of emerging technology. But I believe I can connect the relevant people/business/projects/problems as I am spending many years uploading news videos related to emerging technologies. I thought about creating some kind of web platform to connect the Science and Business worlds. But I postponed this plan as I expect it will be a challenge to bring users to that platform initially. So, currently I am planning to promote my YouTube channel to get more subscribers. Once after getting huge number of subscribers, I believe it will be easy to get users to that connection platform. So, I am running Google Ads to promote the channel.

As I am working on full time for video creation and promotion, I felt that just depending on YouTube alone will be risky as it may do demonetization at any time without any warning or proper explanation as it did two times previously. So, I explored various alternatives for YouTube. Finally I found the Blockchain-based Video platform Odysee which is trying to be the "YouTube of Web3.0".

I came to know that we can earn money from video views on our Odysee channel. Especially, I was told that we can do it without spending much time/effort. We need to just sync our YouTube channel with Odysee channel. It made me to choose Odysee. But Odysee Earnings will be in its own Crypto coin LBRY Credit (LBC) only.

As I am not familiar with Crypto currency usage, I had to go through various articles/videos to learn about Crypto currencies. I came to know that Odysee's Library credit "LBC" is not famous right now. So, only a few Crypto Exchanges are supporting it. But, those Exchanges are not supporting withdrawal into my local bank account. So, I had to find out two Crypto Exchanges. One Exchange for depositing LBC from Odysee and convert it into famous crypto coins like Bitcoin (BTC). The second Exchange is for depositing the famous coin (e.g BTC) from the first crypto Exchange, and for converting it into my local currency for withdrawing it into by bank account. After doing a lot of analysis, I sorted out two exchanges, and did the accounts setup. I will try the LBC withdrawal from Odysee once after earning significant LBC Credits.

Apart from Odysee, I am exploring other blockchain based social networks like Dtube, steemit, hive, etc. As of now, these blockchain platforms are NOT effective.

Though I am not earning much online, I thought sharing my experiences may be helpful for someone willing to start earning online. If you are really willing to focus on your work and maintain integrity, surely you can start earning money online. Don't be greedy, otherwise you will be getting cheated by scams. If you are good at your specific skills or have any good products with competitive price, you can easily get paying customers by putting some efforts for creating your profile, showcasing your skills or product details, doing social media promotion, and running some effective ad campaigns.

Earn from Emerging Technologies

While it may seem easier to make money or conduct business by utilizing emerging technologies, it's important to acknowledge that there are potential risks and challenges involved. Although there may be less competition and ample opportunities, the potential for failure is high due to the untested nature of new technologies. Additionally, potential customers may be hesitant to adopt these emerging technologies, and the technology itself may fail due to a lack of resources or the emergence of superior alternatives. So, always start simple, don't invest much. Instead, grow your business step by step without spending more money.

Initially you may just start with info products as I am doing, like running youTube channel, selling ebook and publishing blogs for giving details about your favorite technology. By doing so, you earn some money and you can use it as a base for your further business initiative. Because, for doing any kind of business, we need to have a content marketing strategy. For example, if you are interested in Graphene, you can start a blog for telling about graphene, you can run a YouTube channel for explaining graphene and for giving latest news about graphene, and you can write an ebook about graphene to sell it thought various ways, like Amazon, Smashwords, etc. Even you can sell them through your blog also using paypal. Later on once you decide to develop any graphene application or graphene production, you can find it easy to sell them once after you develop a huge user base interested in graphene.
I am telling Graphene as an example. You can explore about various opportunities available with different kind of Emerging technologies. In case of AI, you can start with blog, YouTube and ebook approach, then later on, you can earn money by teaching AI

to the people who are interested to learn it, and you can earn money from by developing AI applications also.

Apart from earning money directly from emerging technologies, we can improve our earnings from current work by utilizing emerging technologies effectively. For example, people can reduce their work load heavily by utilizing AI tools properly. For example, chatGPT can help in various ways.

In recent years, numerous businesses, both large and small, have adopted Digital Transformation as a fundamental principle. The Covid19 pandemic has further accelerated this trend for many organizations. The driving forces behind these digital initiatives are the competitive pressures, increasing customer expectations, and the potential for revenue growth. The integration of emerging technologies like Cloud Computing, Machine Learning, Artificial Intelligence, Internet of Things (IoT), and Blockchain has been instrumental in facilitating these digital transformations. So, take necessary steps to keep up yourself according to the digital growth and try to use it effectively for your business growth.

Just explore various emerging technologies like AI, 3D Printing, Brain–computer interface, Nanomedicine, Nanosensors, Self-Healing materials, Quantum dot, carbon nanotubes, Metamaterials, Microfluidics, Magnetic nanoparticles, High-temperature superconductivity, Lab-on-a-chip, Graphene, Conductive polymers, Bioplastic, Aerogel, Vertical farming, Cultured meat, Artificial general intelligence, Flexible electronics, Li-Fi, Machine vision, Memristor, Neuromorphic computing, Quantum computing, Spintronics, Speech recognition, Twistronics, Three-dimensional integrated circuit, virtual reality, Holography, Optical transistor, Screenless display, Artificial photosynthesis, Fusion power, Gravity battery, Lithium–air battery, Lithium–sulfur battery, Nanowire battery, Smart grid, Space-based solar power,

Wireless energy transfer, Superalloy, Artificial uterus, Neuroprosthetics, Flying car, Magnetic levitation, Self-driving car, Space elevator, Hoverbike, Maglev train, Blockchain,etc

While exploring these technologies, make sure that you are reading or watching the content that are based on science research, not based on fiction. You may watch my YouTube channel where I am uploading a lot of tech news videos based on research papers. Once after getting some basic idea of these things, just pick one or two things that are more relevant to your field, career, business, passion, etc. Then put all your efforts to learn more about your chosen technologies. Actively participate in various social media and forum discussions about them, and you may attend any events related to your chosen technologies. It is better to write your learnings as blog posts or upload as videos. It will be helping you to learn better, and you will get opportunity to find like-minded people for possible collaborations, and even you can earn money by showing ads. While doing these things, you will be in a position to develop your product or choose the most suitable product in the market. Then start working on selling your own product or affiliate product to earn money from it. You need to be very much focused now. You may face many difficulties and setbacks. Instead of thinking about changing the product/field/technology frequently, you need to be very strong in selling your product by exploring various opportunities, especially you need to make use of the digital marketing properly. Build up a strong following in all social media sites. Use paid promotions effectively. Continuously optimize your campaigns till you reach positive ROI. Do the proper lead capturing and follow up.

Use Digital marketing effectively

To use digital marketing effectively for your online business, consider the following steps:

Define your target audience: Understand who your target audience is and what they're looking for. I would say that many businesses fail as they are not doing their business activities by keeping their target audiences in mind. For example, I set my target audience for my YouTube channel as english-understandable people who are interested in technology. If I start uploading videos in non-english language, will affect my channel heavily. So, we need to define our target audience properly and we align our activities based on them.

Develop a comprehensive digital marketing strategy: Identify the different channels that you will use to reach your audience, such as social media, email, search engines, and content marketing.

Optimize your website: Ensure that your website is optimized for search engines, is mobile-friendly, and has a clear call-to-action.

Produce valuable content: Create content that is informative, engaging, and relevant to your audience.

Leverage social media: Use social media platforms to connect with your audience, build brand awareness, and drive traffic to your website.

Use paid advertising: Consider using paid advertising to increase your reach and target specific audiences. Personally I like Google Ads PPC campaigns. We need to choose proper keywords, max CPC, etc properly. And, we should continuously tweak our campaigns.

Analyze your results: Use data analytics to track your performance and adjust your strategy accordingly.

By following these steps, you can effectively leverage digital marketing to grow your online business.

Risks of Conducting Business with Emerging Technologies

Emerging technologies have the potential to revolutionize the way we do business, but they also carry some risks that should be considered before investing resources in them. Here are some of the main risks associated with doing business with emerging technologies:

Uncertainty: Emerging technologies are by definition new and untested, which means there is a great deal of uncertainty about how they will perform in the real world. It can be difficult to predict how a new technology will impact your business, or whether it will be successful at all.

Investment risk: Investing in emerging technologies can be risky, as it often involves a significant amount of capital investment upfront. There is no guarantee that the technology will be successful, or that it will provide a return on investment.

Security risk: Many emerging technologies, such as artificial intelligence, the Internet of Things (IoT), and blockchain, involve the collection and sharing of sensitive data. This creates security risks, as there is a potential for data breaches and cyber attacks.

Regulatory risk: Emerging technologies often operate in a legal grey area, as regulations have not yet caught up with the pace of technological change. This can create uncertainty and risk for businesses, as they may not know how to comply with regulations or how regulatory changes may impact their operations.

Scalability risk: Some emerging technologies may work well on a small scale, but may not be able to scale up to meet the needs of larger businesses. This can be a problem if a company invests in a technology that cannot keep up with its growth.

Ethical risk: Emerging technologies can raise ethical concerns, such as the impact of automation on jobs, the use of artificial intelligence in decision-making, or the potential for bias in algorithms. Businesses need to consider these ethical issues when investing in new technologies.

Overall, while emerging technologies offer exciting new opportunities for businesses, it is important to carefully consider the risks before investing in them. Companies should conduct thorough research and due diligence to ensure they are making informed decisions, and should be prepared to adapt their strategies as the technology evolves.

Key Emerging Technologies

Find below some key emerging technologies. There is no significance in the order, I am just listing them in random order.

Artificial Intelligence (AI)

AI refers to the ability of machines or computers to perform tasks that typically require human intelligence, such as visual perception, speech recognition, decision-making, and language translation.

AI is achieved through the development of algorithms and computer programs that enable machines to learn from data and make decisions based on that data. These algorithms are designed to simulate cognitive functions such as learning, reasoning, and problem-solving, and can be used in a wide variety of applications, including healthcare, finance, manufacturing, transportation, and entertainment.

There are different types of AI, including rule-based systems, machine learning, and deep learning. Rule-based systems use a set of predefined rules to make decisions or take actions, while machine learning algorithms can learn from data without being explicitly programmed. Deep learning is a type of machine learning that uses artificial neural networks to learn from large amounts of data, and it has been particularly successful in applications such as image recognition and natural language processing.

AI has the potential to transform many industries and improve people's lives in various ways, but it also raises ethical and social issues, such as the potential loss of jobs to automation, privacy concerns, and biases in algorithms. As AI technology continues to evolve and advance, it is important to consider these implications and develop responsible and ethical approaches to its development and use.

I have uploaded more than 250 videos related to AI innovations on my YouTube Channel.

AI is currently being used in a wide range of applications and industries. Here are some examples:

Healthcare: AI is being used to improve patient outcomes by analyzing medical images, identifying disease patterns, and developing personalized treatment plans. For example, AI can analyze medical scans to help detect cancer earlier, or analyze patient data to identify individuals who are at higher risk of developing certain diseases.

Finance: AI is being used to detect fraudulent transactions, manage portfolios, and develop trading strategies. For example, AI can analyze financial data to identify patterns and trends that humans might miss, and use that information to make more informed investment decisions.

Manufacturing: AI is being used to improve efficiency and productivity in factories by automating processes, predicting equipment failures, and optimizing supply chains. For example, AI can analyze data from sensors on machines to predict when maintenance is needed, or use predictive modeling to optimize the production line.

Retail: AI is being used to personalize shopping experiences, recommend products, and optimize pricing strategies. For example, AI can analyze customer data to make personalized recommendations, or use predictive modeling to determine the optimal price for a product based on demand.

Transportation: AI is being used to improve safety and efficiency in transportation systems, including self-driving cars and drones. For example, AI can analyze sensor data to help cars navigate and avoid accidents, or optimize delivery routes for drones.

These are just a few examples of the many ways that AI is currently being used. As the technology continues to evolve, it is likely that we will see even more widespread adoption and integration of AI in various industries and applications.

Apart from these current uses of AI, the potential uses of AI in the future are vast and exciting. Here are some possible scenarios:

Autonomous Systems: AI will enable autonomous systems, such as self-driving cars, drones, and robots, to become more prevalent and sophisticated. This will lead to safer and more efficient transportation and manufacturing, and enable new applications in fields such as construction, exploration, and emergency response.

Healthcare: AI has the potential to revolutionize healthcare by enabling personalized medicine, faster drug discovery, and remote patient monitoring. AI algorithms could analyze large amounts of data from medical records, imaging, and genomic sequencing to identify patterns and predict disease outcomes.

Education: AI could transform education by enabling personalized learning experiences for students, identifying gaps in learning, and providing real-time feedback to teachers. AI could also facilitate more effective training and professional development for educators.

Entertainment: AI will enable new forms of entertainment, such as virtual reality and augmented reality experiences, that are personalized to individual users. AI could also be used to create more realistic and engaging video games and films.

Environment: AI will enable more accurate and efficient monitoring and management of natural resources and ecosystems. AI could analyze satellite imagery to predict natural disasters, or monitor water quality and air pollution in real-time.

3D Printing

3D printing, also known as additive manufacturing, is a process of creating three-dimensional objects from a digital file by layering materials on top of each other. The process typically involves creating a digital 3D model of the object using computer-aided design (CAD) software, then using a 3D printer to create the physical object.

The 3D printing process can use a variety of materials, including plastics, metals, ceramics, and even living cells. The type of material used depends on the desired properties of the final object, such as strength, flexibility, or conductivity.

3D printing has many potential applications, including:

Prototyping: 3D printing is often used to create prototypes of new products, allowing designers to test and refine their designs before going into mass production.

Manufacturing: 3D printing can be used for small-scale manufacturing of customized products, such as dental implants or hearing aids. It can also be used for on-demand production of replacement parts, reducing the need for large inventories of spare parts.

Education: 3D printing can be used in educational settings to teach students about design and engineering, and to create physical models of complex concepts that are difficult to visualize.

Healthcare: 3D printing can be used to create customized medical implants and prosthetics, tailored to the specific needs of individual patients. It can also be used to create models of patient anatomy for surgical planning.

Art and Design: 3D printing has opened up new possibilities for artists and designers, enabling the creation of complex and intricate sculptures, jewelry, and other objects that would be difficult or impossible to create using traditional manufacturing techniques.

Overall, 3D printing has the potential to revolutionize many industries and enable new applications that were previously impossible. As the technology continues to evolve and become more accessible, it is likely that we will see even more innovative uses of 3D printing in the future.

Brain–computer interface

A brain-computer interface (BCI), also known as a brain-machine interface (BMI), is a technology that enables communication between the brain and a computer or other external device. The goal of a BCI is to allow individuals to control devices or communicate without the need for traditional input methods such as a keyboard or mouse.

BCIs work by detecting and interpreting brain activity, usually through the use of electroencephalography (EEG) sensors placed on the scalp or directly on the brain. The brain signals are then processed and translated into commands that can be used to control external devices, such as prosthetic limbs or computers.

BCIs have many potential applications, including:

Medical Rehabilitation: BCIs can be used to help individuals with disabilities, such as spinal cord injuries or amputations, to control prosthetic limbs and regain mobility.

Communication: BCIs can be used to enable individuals with communication disabilities, such as ALS or cerebral palsy, to communicate using a computer or other external device.

Gaming and Entertainment: BCIs can be used to create more immersive gaming experiences, allowing players to control games using their thoughts or emotions.

Education and Research: BCIs can be used in educational and research settings to study brain function and to teach students about neuroscience and technology.

Military and Security: BCIs have potential applications in military and security settings, such as enabling soldiers to control equipment without using their hands.

While BCIs have many potential benefits, there are also many ethical and practical considerations that must be addressed, such as ensuring the privacy and security of brain data and addressing the potential risks of brain stimulation. Despite these challenges, BCIs are a rapidly developing field with the potential to revolutionize the way we interact with technology and each other.

Nanomedicine

Nanomedicine is a field of medicine that involves the use of nanotechnology, which is the engineering of materials and devices on a nanometer scale, to diagnose, treat, and prevent disease. The application of nanotechnology to medicine has the potential to revolutionize healthcare by enabling targeted and personalized therapies, improving drug delivery, and providing new diagnostic tools.

Nanomedicine involves the use of nanoparticles, which are particles that are between 1 and 100 nanometers in size. These particles can be engineered to have specific properties, such as the ability to target specific cells or tissues in the body, or to release drugs in a controlled manner. Nanoparticles can be made from a variety of materials, including metals, polymers, and lipids.

Nanomedicine has many potential applications, including:

Cancer Therapy: Nanoparticles can be designed to specifically target cancer cells, delivering drugs directly to the tumor while minimizing damage to healthy tissue.

Diagnostics: Nanoparticles can be used as diagnostic tools, such as in imaging techniques that use nanoparticles to highlight specific tissues or organs.

Drug Delivery: Nanoparticles can be used to improve drug delivery, allowing drugs to be delivered directly to the site of action in a controlled and sustained manner.

Regenerative Medicine: Nanoparticles can be used to stimulate tissue regeneration, such as by delivering growth factors or other signaling molecules to damaged tissues.

Vaccines: Nanoparticles can be used to improve the efficacy of vaccines, by delivering antigens directly to immune cells and stimulating a stronger immune response.

Despite the many potential benefits of nanomedicine, there are also potential risks and challenges associated with the use of nanoparticles, such as toxicity and the potential for unintended effects on the body. As such, ongoing research is necessary to ensure the safety and effectiveness of nanomedicine therapies.

Nanosensors

Nanosensors are small-scale devices that can detect and respond to changes in their environment at the nanoscale level. They are used in a wide range of applications, including medicine, environmental monitoring, and electronics.

The most common types of nanosensors include those that rely on changes in electrical properties, optical properties, and chemical properties. For example, some nanosensors can detect changes in electrical conductivity when they are exposed to certain chemicals, while others can measure changes in light absorption or fluorescence.

One major advantage of nanosensors is their small size, which allows them to be used in very small spaces or even inside living cells. This has led to their use in medical applications such as detecting cancer cells or monitoring glucose levels in diabetic patients.

Another advantage of nanosensors is their high sensitivity, which allows them to detect very small changes in their environment. This makes them useful for monitoring environmental pollutants, detecting pathogens in food, and even detecting explosives.

Overall, nanosensors have the potential to revolutionize many industries and improve our ability to detect and respond to changes in our environment. However, there are also concerns about the potential impact of nanosensors on human health and the environment, and more research is needed to fully understand their capabilities and limitations.

Self-Healing materials

Self-healing materials are a class of materials that have the ability to repair damage or defects that occur over time, without the need for human intervention. These materials can be made from a variety of substances, including polymers, metals, ceramics, and composites.

There are several ways in which self-healing materials can function. Some materials have the ability to repair themselves through chemical reactions when they come into contact with a particular stimulus, such as heat or light. Others contain microcapsules filled with healing agents that are released when the material is damaged. Still, others use networks of fibers or polymers that can re-form after being broken.

The potential applications of self-healing materials are vast and varied. For example, in the automotive industry, self-healing materials could be used to repair scratches and dents on car bodies, reducing the need for costly repairs. In the construction industry, self-healing concrete could be used to repair cracks and other damage to buildings, increasing their lifespan and reducing maintenance costs.

In addition to their practical applications, self-healing materials also have the potential to reduce waste and improve sustainability by extending the lifespan of products and reducing the need for replacement materials.

While self-healing materials are a promising technology, there are still challenges to overcome before they can be widely adopted. For example, the cost and complexity of producing these materials are currently high, and there is a need for further research to optimize their properties and performance.

Quantum dot

Quantum dots are tiny particles made up of semiconductor materials that are only a few nanometers in size. They have unique electronic and optical properties that make them useful in a wide range of applications, including electronics, biomedicine, and energy.

The size of a quantum dot is so small that it causes quantum confinement of electrons, which gives them unique optical and electrical properties. Specifically, quantum dots exhibit fluorescence, meaning they can absorb and emit light at specific wavelengths, which can be tuned by changing the size of the particle. This property makes quantum dots useful in applications such as medical imaging and LED displays.

Quantum dots are also being explored for use in quantum computing, a type of computing that uses quantum mechanics to perform calculations. Because of their small size and unique electronic properties, quantum dots can be used as qubits, the basic units of quantum computing. Quantum dots are being developed as qubits that can be controlled and manipulated using electric and magnetic fields, making them a promising technology for quantum computing.

However, there are also concerns about the potential health and environmental impacts of quantum dots, as they contain heavy metals such as cadmium and lead. Research is ongoing to understand these potential risks and to develop safer forms of quantum dots.

Overall, quantum dots are a promising area of research with many potential applications. However, more research is needed to optimize their properties, improve their safety, and develop new applications.

Carbon nanotubes

Carbon nanotubes are cylindrical structures made up of carbon atoms arranged in a hexagonal lattice. They have unique electronic, mechanical, and thermal properties that make them useful in a wide range of applications, including electronics, materials science, and biomedicine.

Carbon nanotubes are incredibly strong and stiff, with a tensile strength many times that of steel. They are also highly conductive, which makes them useful in electronics and energy storage. Additionally, their small size and high aspect ratio make them useful as reinforcements in composite materials.

In biomedicine, carbon nanotubes are being explored for use in drug delivery and tissue engineering due to their ability to penetrate cell membranes and their biocompatibility. However, there are also concerns about the potential toxicity of carbon nanotubes, and research is ongoing to understand and mitigate these risks.

Carbon nanotubes have also shown promise in applications such as nanoelectronics, where they are being explored as potential components in smaller, faster, and more efficient devices. Additionally, carbon nanotubes have potential applications in energy storage, where their high surface area and conductivity make them useful in supercapacitors and batteries.

Despite their promising properties, there are still challenges to overcome in the development and application of carbon nanotubes. These include improving the scalability and cost-effectiveness of production methods and addressing concerns about their potential toxicity and environmental impact. Nonetheless, carbon nanotubes remain a highly active area of research and development.

Metamaterials

Metamaterials are artificially engineered materials that have properties not found in natural materials. They are made up of specially designed structures that manipulate electromagnetic waves, sound waves, and other types of waves in ways that are not possible with natural materials.

One of the most common types of metamaterials is known as a negative index material, which has a negative refractive index. This means that it can bend light in the opposite direction of conventional materials. Negative index materials have the potential to create lenses that can focus light to a resolution much smaller than the wavelength of the light, which could have implications for high-resolution imaging and communication technologies.

Metamaterials can also be designed to exhibit other unusual properties, such as perfect absorption, cloaking, and superlensing. Perfect absorption metamaterials can absorb nearly all of the electromagnetic radiation that falls upon them, while cloaking metamaterials can redirect light or other waves around an object, making it invisible. Superlensing metamaterials can go beyond the diffraction limit and provide subwavelength resolution.

Metamaterials have a wide range of potential applications, including in optics, telecommunications, sensing, and energy. For example, metamaterials could be used to improve the performance of solar cells by manipulating the way light is absorbed and transmitted within the material. They could also be used to create more efficient sensors by enhancing the sensitivity and selectivity of the sensing material.

Despite their potential, metamaterials are still a relatively new area of research, and there are many challenges to overcome before they can be widely used in practical applications. These challenges include improving the scalability and cost-effectiveness of production methods and developing a better understanding of the potential environmental and health impacts of these materials. Nonetheless, the unique properties of metamaterials make them a promising area of research with many potential applications.

Microfluidics

Microfluidics is a field of research that deals with the behavior, control, and manipulation of fluids and particles at the microscale level, typically in the range of micrometers to millimeters. Microfluidic devices are characterized by their small size and the ability to precisely control fluid flows and transport, making them useful for a wide range of applications, including biomedical analysis, chemical synthesis, and environmental monitoring.

Microfluidic devices typically use channels and chambers etched or fabricated on a chip, which can be made from materials such as glass, silicon, or polymers. These channels and chambers can be designed to carry out specific tasks, such as mixing and separating fluids, performing chemical reactions, or analyzing biological samples.

Microfluidics has the potential to revolutionize a number of fields, including medical diagnostics, drug development, and environmental monitoring, by enabling more precise and efficient manipulation of fluids and particles at a smaller scale than is possible with traditional techniques.

Magnetic nanoparticles

Magnetic nanoparticles are a type of nanoparticle that have magnetic properties. They are typically composed of magnetic materials such as iron, cobalt, nickel, or their alloys and have a size range of about 1-100 nanometers.

Magnetic nanoparticles have a variety of applications in fields such as biomedicine, environmental monitoring, and data storage. In biomedicine, magnetic nanoparticles can be used for targeted drug delivery, magnetic hyperthermia treatment of cancer, magnetic resonance imaging (MRI) contrast agents, and biosensors. In environmental monitoring, they can be used for water purification and environmental remediation. In data storage, they can be used for high-density magnetic recording.

The magnetic properties of these nanoparticles are due to the presence of unpaired electrons in their atomic or molecular orbitals, which create a magnetic moment. The size and shape of the nanoparticles can influence their magnetic properties, such as magnetic anisotropy, which can affect their usefulness in different applications.

Magnetic nanoparticles can be synthesized using various methods, including chemical precipitation, thermal decomposition, and sol-gel synthesis. Surface modification of the nanoparticles with biocompatible materials is often necessary for biomedical applications to prevent aggregation and enhance stability in biological environments.

High-temperature superconductivity

High-temperature superconductivity (HTS) refers to the phenomenon of materials exhibiting zero electrical resistance at temperatures higher than the boiling point of liquid nitrogen

(-196°C). This is in contrast to traditional superconductors, which typically require temperatures close to absolute zero (-273°C) to exhibit zero electrical resistance.

The discovery of high-temperature superconductivity in the 1980s sparked great interest in the scientific community due to its potential for practical applications, such as more efficient electrical transmission and energy storage. However, the mechanism behind high-temperature superconductivity is not yet fully understood, and research in this field is ongoing.

The most common types of high-temperature superconductors are copper-based compounds (known as cuprates) and iron-based compounds. These materials have complex crystal structures that contribute to their unique electrical properties. The exact mechanism behind high-temperature superconductivity is still a subject of debate, but it is believed to be related to the interactions between the electrons in the material and the lattice vibrations of the crystal structure.

Despite the challenges of working with high-temperature superconductors, research in this field has continued to advance. Scientists have made progress in developing new materials with even higher superconducting temperatures, as well as understanding the mechanisms behind high-temperature superconductivity. Potential applications of high-temperature superconductivity include more efficient electrical transmission and energy storage, high-speed transportation systems such as maglev trains, and powerful electromagnets for scientific research.

Lab-on-a-chip

Lab-on-a-chip (LOC) is a miniaturized device that integrates various laboratory functions onto a single microchip. These devices are typically used for chemical or biological analysis, and they enable rapid and precise testing of small sample volumes with high sensitivity and specificity.

LOC devices typically consist of channels, chambers, and valves etched or fabricated on a chip using microfabrication techniques. These channels and chambers can be designed to perform specific functions, such as mixing, separation, detection, and analysis of samples.

The advantages of lab-on-a-chip devices include their small size, low cost, and ability to automate and streamline laboratory processes. LOC devices have a wide range of applications in fields such as biomedical research, clinical diagnostics, environmental monitoring, and food safety testing.

In biomedical research, LOC devices are used for high-throughput screening of drug candidates, cellular analysis, and genomics research. In clinical diagnostics, they are used for point-of-care testing, infectious disease detection, and personalized medicine. In environmental monitoring, they are used for monitoring water quality, air pollution, and soil contamination. In food safety testing, they are used for rapid detection of foodborne pathogens and contaminants.

One of the challenges in developing lab-on-a-chip devices is integrating multiple functions onto a single chip without cross-contamination between samples. This requires careful design and optimization of the microfluidic channels and valves, as well as the development of sensitive and specific detection methods. However, advances in microfabrication techniques, nanotechnology, and biosensors continue to drive innovation in this field, making lab-on-a-chip devices increasingly powerful and useful tools for scientific research and practical applications.

Graphene

Graphene is a two-dimensional material composed of a single layer of carbon atoms arranged in a hexagonal lattice. It is the basic building block of other carbon-based materials such as graphite, carbon nanotubes, and fullerenes.

Graphene has attracted considerable attention due to its unique electrical, mechanical, and thermal properties. It is one of the strongest materials known, with a tensile strength more than 100 times greater than steel. It also has high electrical conductivity and mobility, as well as high thermal conductivity.

The unique properties of graphene make it attractive for a wide range of applications, including electronics, energy storage, sensors, and biomedical devices. In electronics, graphene can be used to create high-performance transistors, displays, and touchscreens. In energy storage, graphene can be used as an electrode material for batteries and supercapacitors, which could lead to higher energy densities and faster charging times. In sensors, graphene can be used for gas sensing and biosensing applications due to its high surface area and sensitivity to changes in its environment. In biomedical devices, graphene can be used for drug delivery, tissue engineering, and imaging.

Graphene can be synthesized using various methods, including mechanical exfoliation, chemical vapor deposition, and solution-based methods. However, the scalability and cost of producing high-quality graphene remain a challenge.

Research on graphene continues to expand, with ongoing efforts to better understand its properties, improve its production methods, and develop new applications for this remarkable material.

Conductive polymers

Conductive polymers are a class of organic materials that can conduct electricity. They are made up of repeating units of small organic molecules or macromolecules, and their conductivity arises from the movement of charged particles (electrons or ions) through the polymer chain.

The electrical conductivity of conductive polymers can be varied over a wide range by adjusting the doping level, which involves the addition or removal of electrons or ions. Doping can be achieved through various means, such as chemical oxidation/reduction, protonation/deprotonation, or exposure to electromagnetic radiation.

Conductive polymers have unique electronic, optical, and mechanical properties that make them attractive for a variety of applications, such as electronic devices, sensors, actuators, and energy storage devices. In electronics, conductive polymers can be used for transistors, light-emitting diodes (LEDs), and solar cells. In sensors and actuators, conductive polymers can be used to detect changes in temperature, pressure, humidity, or chemical composition. In energy storage devices, conductive polymers can be used as electrode materials for batteries and supercapacitors.

One of the advantages of conductive polymers is their low weight, flexibility, and ease of processing. They can be easily molded or shaped into various forms, including thin films, fibers, and coatings. However, one of the challenges of using conductive polymers is their stability and durability under different conditions. They are often sensitive to environmental factors such as moisture, heat, and light, which can degrade their electrical and mechanical properties.

Despite these challenges, research on conductive polymers continues to advance, with ongoing efforts to improve their stability, increase their conductivity, and develop new applications for these versatile materials.

Bioplastic

Bioplastics are a type of plastic that are made from renewable biomass sources, such as vegetable fats and oils, cornstarch, and pea starch, instead of fossil fuels. Bioplastics can be produced using various methods, including fermentation, chemical synthesis, and enzymatic catalysis.

There are two main types of bioplastics: biodegradable and non-biodegradable. Biodegradable bioplastics can be broken down by natural processes into simpler compounds, such as water, carbon dioxide, and biomass. Non-biodegradable bioplastics are made from renewable resources but do not readily decompose in the environment.

Bioplastics have a variety of applications in packaging, agriculture, textiles, and biomedical engineering. In packaging, bioplastics can be used for food containers, bags, and disposable cutlery. In agriculture, bioplastics can be used for mulch films and plant pots. In textiles, bioplastics can be used for clothing, shoes, and bags. In biomedical engineering, bioplastics can be used for drug delivery, tissue engineering, and medical implants.

One of the advantages of bioplastics is their potential to reduce environmental pollution and greenhouse gas emissions. Bioplastics made from renewable sources can reduce dependence on non-renewable resources and reduce the amount of plastic waste that ends up in landfills or oceans. However, the production of bioplastics requires careful consideration of the environmental impacts of the production process, including the use of land, water, and energy resources, as well as the potential for environmental pollution from the use of fertilizers, pesticides, and other inputs.

Aerogel

Aerogel is a synthetic porous material that is composed of a gel in which the liquid component has been replaced with gas, resulting in a solid material that is almost entirely made up of air. Aerogels can be made from various materials, including silica, carbon, and metal oxides, and they are known for their low density, high surface area, and exceptional thermal insulation properties.

Aerogels are some of the lightest materials known, with densities ranging from about 0.001 to 0.5 g/cm^3. They also have high surface areas, which can range from 100 to 1000 square meters per gram, making them attractive for applications in catalysis, sensors, and energy storage. Aerogels are also excellent insulators, with thermal conductivities that are typically one or two orders of magnitude lower than those of other insulating materials.

Aerogels have a wide range of applications, including in aerospace, energy, construction, and environmental remediation. In aerospace, aerogels can be used as lightweight insulation for spacecraft and spacesuits. In energy, aerogels can be used as electrode materials for batteries and supercapacitors, as well as for thermal insulation in buildings and industrial processes. In construction, aerogels can be used as insulation for walls, roofs, and windows. In environmental remediation, aerogels can be used to capture and remove pollutants from air and water.

One of the challenges of using aerogels is their brittleness, which can make them difficult to handle and process. However, researchers are developing new methods to produce aerogels that are more flexible and durable, as well as to scale up their production for commercial applications. Overall, aerogels represent a promising class of materials with unique properties that make them attractive for a wide range of applications.

Vertical farming

Vertical farming is a method of growing crops in vertically stacked layers or shelves, using artificial lighting, controlled temperature and humidity, and precise nutrient delivery systems. This method of farming can be used in both urban and rural settings and is becoming increasingly popular due to its potential to increase crop yield, reduce water usage, and minimize environmental impact.

Vertical farming can take many forms, including indoor farms, greenhouses, and shipping container farms. In these systems, crops are grown hydroponically or aeroponically, meaning that they are grown in nutrient-rich water or air without the use of soil. This allows for greater control over plant growth and can lead to faster growth rates and higher yields than traditional farming methods.

One of the advantages of vertical farming is its ability to produce fresh produce in urban areas, reducing the distance that food has to travel and minimizing the environmental impact of transportation. Vertical farming can also use significantly less water than traditional farming, as water is recycled and reused in closed-loop systems.

Vertical farming also has the potential to be more energy efficient than traditional farming methods, as it can use LED lighting and other technologies to provide precise amounts of light and heat to the crops. Additionally, vertical farming can allow for year-round production, reducing the impact of seasonal variations on crop yield.

Despite these advantages, there are also challenges to vertical farming, including the high initial capital costs of setting up a vertical farm and the need for skilled workers to operate and maintain the systems. However, as technology continues to improve and the demand for locally grown, fresh produce increases, vertical farming is likely to become an increasingly important part of our food system.

Cultured meat

Cultured meat, also known as lab-grown meat or cell-based meat, is a type of meat that is produced by growing animal cells in a lab instead of raising and slaughtering animals. Cultured meat is made by taking a small sample of animal cells, such as muscle cells, and then using biotechnology to replicate those cells and grow them into muscle tissue.

Cultured meat has the potential to offer a more sustainable and ethical alternative to traditional meat production. It requires significantly less land, water, and other resources than traditional animal agriculture, and it has the potential to reduce greenhouse gas emissions and other environmental impacts associated with meat production. Additionally, cultured meat does not involve the slaughter of animals, which may be more ethical and appealing to some consumers.

There are several challenges to producing cultured meat at scale, including the high cost of production and the need for regulatory approval. However, as technology improves and the demand for sustainable and ethical meat alternatives increases, it is likely that cultured meat will become an increasingly important part of our food system.

Cultured meat has the potential to revolutionize the way we produce and consume meat, offering a more sustainable and ethical alternative to traditional animal agriculture. While there are still many challenges to overcome, the growing interest and investment in cultured meat suggest that this technology is likely to play an important role in the future of food production.

Artificial general intelligence (AGI)

Artificial general intelligence (AGI) refers to the ability of a machine or computer program to perform any intellectual task that a human can do. Unlike narrow AI, which is designed to perform specific tasks such as image recognition or language translation, AGI is capable of learning and adapting to new situations, solving problems, and making decisions in a wide range of contexts.

The development of AGI is often seen as the ultimate goal of artificial intelligence research, as it has the potential to fundamentally transform many aspects of our society and economy. An AGI system could be used to solve complex scientific and engineering problems, provide personalized healthcare, manage complex financial systems, and even create new works of art and literature.

However, achieving AGI is a challenging and complex problem. It requires the development of machine learning algorithms and hardware that can replicate the complexity and flexibility of the human brain, as well as the ability to integrate and process vast amounts of data from multiple sources.

Additionally, there are concerns about the potential risks and ethical implications of AGI. As AGI systems become more intelligent and autonomous, there is a risk that they could become uncontrollable or act in ways that are harmful to humans. To address these concerns, researchers and policymakers are exploring ways to ensure that AGI is developed in a safe and ethical manner, with appropriate safeguards and oversight.

Overall, while the development of AGI is still in its early stages, it has the potential to be a transformative technology that could shape the future of our society and economy. However, achieving AGI will require significant advances in machine learning, data processing, and hardware development, as well as careful consideration of the ethical and societal implications of this technology.

Flexible electronics

Flexible electronics refers to electronic devices and circuits that can be bent, twisted, or stretched without breaking or losing their functionality. Unlike traditional rigid electronics, which are made from materials like silicon that are brittle and inflexible, flexible electronics are made from a range of materials that are designed to be more flexible and durable.

Flexible electronics have many potential applications, ranging from wearable health monitors and smart clothing to foldable smartphones and flexible displays. By making electronics more flexible, these devices can be more comfortable and convenient to use, and they can also be made to fit a wider range of body shapes and sizes.

There are several challenges to developing flexible electronics, including the need to develop new materials and manufacturing processes that are capable of producing flexible electronic components at scale. Additionally, there is a need to ensure that flexible electronics are reliable and long-lasting, as they may be subjected to more wear and tear than traditional electronics.

Despite these challenges, flexible electronics are becoming increasingly common in a variety of applications, from medical devices to consumer electronics. As technology continues to improve, it is likely that flexible electronics will become even more versatile and widely used, transforming the way we interact with electronic devices and opening up new opportunities for innovation and creativity.

Li-Fi

Li-Fi, which stands for "Light Fidelity," is a wireless communication technology that uses light to transmit data. Li-Fi works by modulating the light emitted by LED lamps or other light sources, using variations in intensity that are too fast to be detected by the human eye. These variations can be used to transmit data, similar to how radio waves are used in traditional Wi-Fi.

One of the main advantages of Li-Fi is its potential for very high-speed data transmission. Because light can be modulated much more quickly than radio waves, Li-Fi has the potential to achieve much faster data transfer rates than traditional Wi-Fi. Additionally, because light does not penetrate walls and other obstacles as easily as radio waves, Li-Fi can be more secure and less susceptible to interference.

However, there are also some limitations to Li-Fi. Because it relies on direct line-of-sight between the transmitter and receiver, it may not be as suitable for certain types of applications or environments, such as large open spaces or outdoor areas. Additionally, because it relies on light sources such as LED lamps, it may not be as widely available or easy to implement as traditional Wi-Fi.

Despite these challenges, Li-Fi is an exciting technology with the potential to transform the way we communicate and access information. As the technology continues to evolve and improve, it may become a more common and widely used alternative to traditional Wi-Fi in certain applications and environments.

Machine vision

Machine vision, also known as computer vision, is a field of artificial intelligence that focuses on enabling computers to interpret and understand visual information from the world around them.

Machine vision uses various techniques and algorithms to analyze digital images and video in order to recognize objects, detect patterns, and extract useful information.

Machine vision has a wide range of applications, including industrial automation, surveillance and security, medical imaging, and autonomous vehicles. In manufacturing, for example, machine vision systems can be used to inspect products for defects, measure dimensions and tolerances, and monitor production processes for quality control. In medical imaging, machine vision can be used to identify abnormalities in X-rays or MRI scans, helping doctors to make more accurate diagnoses and treatment decisions.

Machine vision systems typically consist of a camera or other imaging device, software algorithms for image processing and analysis, and hardware for data storage and processing. The algorithms used in machine vision may be based on machine learning techniques, such as neural networks or decision trees, which can be trained to recognize specific objects or patterns in images.

One of the challenges of machine vision is dealing with the complexity and variability of visual data. Real-world images may contain variations in lighting, angle, distance, and other factors that can make object recognition and analysis difficult. To overcome these challenges, machine vision researchers are developing new techniques and algorithms that can handle more complex and varied visual data, as well as hardware that can process and analyze visual data more quickly and efficiently.

Memristor

A memristor is a two-terminal electronic device that can change its resistance based on the history of the electrical signals that have been applied to it. In other words, it "remembers" the electrical state it was in the last time it was used.

The memristor was first theorized in 1971 by Leon Chua, a professor of electrical engineering and computer science at the University of California, Berkeley. However, it wasn't until 2008 that the first practical memristor was developed by a team of researchers at HP Labs.

Memristors have several potential applications in electronics, including as a replacement for traditional storage devices such as hard drives and flash memory. Memristors have the potential to be faster, more energy-efficient, and more durable than traditional storage devices, and they may also be able to store more data in a smaller physical space.

In addition to storage applications, memristors may also be used in neural networks and other types of artificial intelligence applications. Memristors can be used to model the way that biological neurons work, which could help to develop more efficient and accurate AI systems.

Despite their potential advantages, there are still some challenges to developing practical memristors for widespread use. One of the main challenges is developing manufacturing techniques that can produce memristors in large quantities and at a reasonable cost. Nonetheless, memristors are an active area of research and development, and they may play an increasingly important role in the future of electronics and computing.

Neuromorphic computing

Neuromorphic computing is a field of computer engineering that aims to design computer systems that mimic the behavior of the human brain. This type of computing is based on the principles of neuroscience and seeks to create systems that can process and analyze large amounts of data in a way that is more similar to the way the human brain works.

One of the key features of neuromorphic computing is the use of artificial neural networks. These networks are composed of interconnected nodes that are modeled after the neurons found in the human brain. Each node, or artificial neuron, is capable of processing information and communicating with other nodes through a series of electrical signals.

Neuromorphic computing also incorporates elements of parallel processing and event-driven computing, which enable the system to process large amounts of data quickly and efficiently. Additionally, neuromorphic systems are designed to be highly adaptable and can learn and evolve over time, similar to the way the human brain can change and adapt based on new experiences.

Neuromorphic computing has many potential applications, including in the fields of robotics, image and speech recognition, and natural language processing. For example, neuromorphic systems could be used to create robots that can learn and adapt to their environment, or to develop more advanced systems for analyzing and interpreting medical data.

Overall, neuromorphic computing represents a promising area of research that has the potential to revolutionize the way we approach computing and data analysis.

Quantum computing

Quantum computing is a field of computing that utilizes the principles of quantum mechanics to perform operations and solve problems that are difficult or impossible for classical computers to handle. Unlike classical computers, which use bits to represent data and perform calculations, quantum computers use quantum bits or qubits, which can exist in multiple states simultaneously.

One of the key advantages of quantum computing is its ability to perform calculations at a much faster rate than classical computers. This is because quantum computers can perform many calculations simultaneously, thanks to the principle of superposition, which allows qubits to exist in multiple states at once. Additionally, quantum computers can use a technique called entanglement, which allows multiple qubits to be linked together in such a way that the state of one qubit is dependent on the state of the other.

Quantum computing has many potential applications, including in the fields of cryptography, optimization, and machine learning. For example, quantum computers could be used to develop more secure encryption algorithms, or to optimize complex logistical problems that would be too difficult for classical computers to handle.

However, there are also significant challenges associated with quantum computing. One of the biggest challenges is the issue of quantum decoherence, which occurs when qubits lose their quantum state due to interaction with their environment. Additionally, quantum computers require very specific and controlled environments to operate, which can make them expensive and difficult to build and maintain.

Despite these challenges, the field of quantum computing is rapidly advancing, and many researchers and companies are investing in the development of quantum computing technology. As these technologies continue to evolve, they have the potential to fundamentally transform the way we approach computing and problem-solving.

Spintronics

Spintronics, also known as spin electronics, is a field of study in electronics and physics that aims to exploit the spin of electrons for use in electronic devices. Unlike conventional electronics, which rely on the charge of electrons to encode information, spintronics uses the intrinsic spin of electrons to store and manipulate data.

In spintronics, the spin of electrons is used to represent binary information, with up-spin electrons representing a "1" and down-spin electrons representing a "0". This allows for the creation of non-volatile, low-power memory devices that do not rely on the constant flow of electric current to maintain their state.

Spintronics has the potential to revolutionize the electronics industry by enabling the creation of faster, smaller, and more energy-efficient devices. It has already been used in hard disk drives to increase their storage capacity and in magnetic random-access memory (MRAM) to create low-power, high-speed memory.

Other potential applications of spintronics include spin-based logic devices, spin-based sensors, and spin-based quantum computers. Spintronics also has implications for the study of fundamental physics, as it allows researchers to study the behavior of spin in materials at the nanoscale.

While spintronics is still a relatively new field, it has already shown great promise and is expected to continue to grow in importance in the coming years.

Speech recognition

Speech recognition is a technology that enables computers or devices to recognize and interpret spoken language. It uses algorithms and machine learning techniques to convert human speech into digital signals that can be understood by a computer.

Speech recognition is used in a wide range of applications, from voice assistants like Siri and Alexa to automated customer service systems, medical transcriptions, and language translation. It is particularly useful for individuals who have difficulty typing, such as those with physical disabilities or those who need to transcribe large amounts of audio.

The process of speech recognition involves several steps, including acoustic analysis, feature extraction, acoustic modeling, language modeling, and decoding. During the acoustic analysis stage, the system processes the audio input and extracts features such as pitch, duration, and intensity. The acoustic model then uses this information to identify phonemes, the basic units of sound in a language. The language model analyzes the sequence of phonemes to determine the most likely word or phrase being spoken, and the decoding stage produces the final output.

While speech recognition technology has come a long way in recent years, it still has limitations. Accurately recognizing speech can be challenging in noisy environments or when dealing with accents, dialects, or unusual speech patterns. However, ongoing advances in machine learning and natural language processing are helping to improve the accuracy and effectiveness of speech recognition technology.

Twistronics

Twistronics is a field of study in materials science and physics that involves manipulating the twist angle between two layers of two-dimensional materials, such as graphene or transition metal dichalcogenides (TMDs). By changing the angle at which these layers are stacked, it is possible to alter the electronic properties of the materials in a precise and controllable way.

The term "twistronics" was first introduced in a 2018 paper by researchers at the Massachusetts Institute of Technology (MIT), who demonstrated that by adjusting the twist angle between two layers of graphene, they could create a new type of superconductor that exhibits unique electronic properties.

One of the key features of twistronics is that it allows for the creation of what are known as "magic angles," where the twist angle between two layers of material is precisely tuned to create new electronic states. These magic angles can give rise to phenomena such as superconductivity, where a material can conduct electricity with zero resistance, or Mott insulators, where a material that would normally conduct electricity becomes an insulator.

Twistronics has the potential to revolutionize the field of electronics by allowing for the creation of new materials with unique electronic properties that could be used in a variety of applications, such as in ultrafast electronic devices or in quantum computing. However, there is still much to be learned about the fundamental physics of twistronics, and research in this field is ongoing.

Three-dimensional integrated circuit

A three-dimensional integrated circuit (3D IC) is a type of integrated circuit (IC) that involves stacking multiple layers of electronic components, such as transistors and memory cells, on top of one another to create a three-dimensional structure. This approach allows for a greater number of components to be packed into a smaller space, resulting in faster and more efficient circuits.

In a traditional two-dimensional IC, the components are arranged side by side on a single plane. However, as the number of components in an IC increases, the size of the chip can become a limiting factor, as the distances between components must be large enough to avoid interference and crosstalk. By stacking components vertically in a 3D IC, the distances between components can be reduced, allowing for faster communication and reduced power consumption.

There are several different types of 3D ICs, including through-silicon vias (TSVs), which are vertical interconnects that allow for communication between different layers of the IC. Another type of 3D IC is the monolithic 3D IC, which involves growing layers of components on top of one another, rather than stacking pre-fabricated components.

3D ICs have several advantages over traditional ICs, including increased speed, reduced power consumption, and reduced form factor. They are particularly well-suited for applications such as high-performance computing, data centers, and mobile devices.

However, there are also some challenges associated with 3D ICs, including increased complexity in design and manufacturing, as well as potential issues with heat dissipation and reliability. Nonetheless, ongoing research in this field is helping to overcome these challenges and improve the performance and efficiency of 3D ICs.

Virtual reality (VR) / Augmented Reality (AR)

Virtual reality (VR) and augmented reality (AR) are two related but distinct technologies that have become increasingly popular in recent years. Both involve the use of computer-generated content to create immersive experiences, but they differ in terms of how that content is presented and how users interact with it.

Virtual reality (VR) is a technology that uses head-mounted displays and other hardware to create a fully immersive digital environment that simulates a real-world experience. The user is typically completely cut off from the real world and is fully immersed in the virtual environment. This technology is often used in gaming, training simulations, and other applications where a highly immersive experience is desired.

Augmented reality (AR), on the other hand, involves overlaying digital content onto the real world, typically using a smartphone or other mobile device. This technology allows users to see and interact with virtual objects and information in the real world. AR is often used in applications such as gaming, navigation, and marketing.

Both VR and AR have numerous applications across a wide range of industries, including entertainment, education, healthcare, and retail. In education and training, for example, VR and AR can be used to simulate real-world scenarios and provide hands-on experience in a safe and controlled environment. In healthcare, these technologies can be used for surgical training, pain management, and other applications.

While VR and AR offer many benefits, there are also some challenges associated with these technologies, including the need for specialized hardware and software, potential issues with motion sickness in VR, and privacy concerns in AR. Nonetheless, ongoing advances in technology and increased adoption of these technologies are helping to address these challenges and make VR and AR more accessible to a wider audience.

Mixed reality (MR) is a term used to describe a type of technology that combines elements of virtual reality (VR) and augmented reality (AR) to create a seamless blend of real and digital environments. MR is sometimes also referred to as hybrid reality or extended reality (XR).

In MR, digital objects are placed within the real world, and users can interact with them in a natural and intuitive way. This is achieved using special hardware, such as head-mounted displays, and sophisticated software that can track the user's movements and adjust the virtual content accordingly. The result is an immersive experience that combines the best aspects of VR and AR.

One of the key advantages of MR is its versatility. Unlike VR, which completely replaces the real world with a digital environment, and AR, which overlays digital content onto the real world, MR can seamlessly blend the two together to create a unique and compelling experience. This opens up a wide range of possibilities for applications across many industries, including gaming, education, healthcare, and more.

In gaming, for example, MR can be used to create interactive experiences that blur the lines between the real and virtual worlds, allowing players to fully immerse themselves in the game. In education, MR can be used to create virtual classrooms and interactive learning environments that enhance student engagement and learning outcomes. In healthcare, MR can be used to simulate complex medical procedures and provide hands-on training for medical professionals.

While MR is still a relatively new technology, it has already shown great promise in a wide range of applications. As the technology continues to evolve and become more sophisticated, it is likely to become an increasingly important tool for enhancing human experiences in many different contexts.

Holography

Holography is a technique used to create three-dimensional images or holograms using lasers. Unlike traditional photographs or images, which are two-dimensional representations of objects or scenes, holograms capture and reproduce the full three-dimensional information of an object or scene. This creates a highly realistic and immersive visual experience that is often compared to the actual object or scene being depicted.

The process of creating a hologram involves splitting a laser beam into two parts - a reference beam and an object beam. The object beam is directed onto the object being imaged, and the light scattered by the object is captured on a photographic plate or other light-sensitive medium. The reference beam is also directed onto the photographic plate, and the interference pattern between the two beams is recorded. When the hologram is illuminated with a laser beam, the recorded interference pattern causes the light to diffract, creating a three-dimensional image of the object.

Holography has many practical applications in a variety of fields, including art, entertainment, and security. In art, holography is used to create highly realistic and immersive visual experiences that can be used to create stunning visual displays and installations. In entertainment, holography is used to create 3D visual effects for movies, television shows, and live performances. In security, holograms are used to create highly secure and tamper-proof documents and other items, such as credit cards and passports.

While holography has many practical applications, it is also a fascinating scientific phenomenon that has been studied for many years. In addition to its applications in imaging and display technology, holography has also contributed to our understanding of quantum mechanics and other areas of physics. As technology continues to advance, it is likely that holography will continue to play an important role in many different fields.

Optical transistor

An optical transistor is a device that controls the flow of light in much the same way that a conventional electronic transistor controls the flow of electricity. Optical transistors are a key component of many advanced optical systems and devices, including optical communication networks, optical sensors, and optical computing.

In an optical transistor, light is used to control the properties of a semiconductor material in much the same way that an electrical current is used to control the properties of a conventional transistor. When light is applied to the transistor, it creates a flow of electrons that can be controlled to produce a desired output. This allows the transistor to act as a switch or amplifier for optical signals, much like a conventional transistor does for electrical signals.

One of the key advantages of optical transistors is their high speed and bandwidth. Because light travels much faster than electricity, optical transistors can switch and process signals at very high speeds, making them ideal for use in high-speed optical communication networks and other advanced optical systems.

Optical transistors are also highly efficient and consume less power than traditional electronic transistors. This makes them ideal for use in low-power devices such as sensors and other battery-powered devices.

While optical transistors are still a relatively new technology, they have already shown great promise in a wide range of applications. As researchers continue to develop new materials and techniques for creating optical transistors, it is likely that these devices will become an increasingly important part of the modern technological landscape, enabling new and innovative optical systems and devices.

Artificial photosynthesis

Artificial photosynthesis is a process that mimics the natural process of photosynthesis, which is the process by which plants and other organisms convert sunlight, water, and carbon dioxide into energy-rich organic compounds such as sugars. Artificial photosynthesis aims to create a similar process using man-made materials and techniques in order to produce renewable fuels and other useful chemicals.

The basic principle of artificial photosynthesis is to use a catalyst to split water molecules into oxygen and hydrogen. The hydrogen can then be used as a fuel or combined with carbon dioxide to produce hydrocarbons or other chemicals. In order to do this, researchers are exploring a variety of different catalysts, such as metal oxides, that can absorb sunlight and catalyze the chemical reactions necessary to split water molecules.

One of the main advantages of artificial photosynthesis is its potential to provide a renewable and sustainable source of energy. By using sunlight to drive the chemical reactions, artificial photosynthesis can produce fuels and chemicals without relying on fossil fuels, which are a finite resource and contribute to climate change.

However, there are still many challenges that must be overcome in order to make artificial photosynthesis a practical and economically viable technology. One of the main challenges is developing efficient and stable catalysts that can effectively split water molecules and produce useful chemicals. Researchers are also exploring ways to integrate artificial photosynthesis into existing energy systems and infrastructure.

Despite these challenges, artificial photosynthesis has the potential to play a key role in the transition to a more sustainable and renewable energy future. As research continues, it is likely that this technology will become increasingly important in the years to come.

Fusion power

Fusion power is a form of energy that is generated by nuclear fusion, which is the process by which two atomic nuclei come together to form a heavier nucleus, releasing energy in the process. Fusion power has the potential to provide a virtually limitless source of clean and sustainable energy.

The basic principle of fusion power is to use the energy released by nuclear fusion to generate heat, which can then be used to produce electricity. To achieve this, researchers are exploring a variety of different methods for achieving controlled nuclear fusion reactions, including magnetic confinement, inertial confinement, and laser-induced fusion.

One of the main advantages of fusion power is its potential to provide a virtually unlimited source of energy. Unlike fossil fuels, which are a finite resource that will eventually run out, the fuel for fusion power - typically hydrogen isotopes such as deuterium and tritium - is abundant and readily available.

Another advantage of fusion power is that it produces no greenhouse gases or other harmful pollutants. Unlike fossil fuels, which emit large amounts of carbon dioxide and other pollutants when burned, fusion power generates no emissions and produces no radioactive waste.

Despite these advantages, there are still many challenges that must be overcome in order to make fusion power a practical and economically viable technology. One of the main challenges is developing efficient and cost-effective fusion reactors that can sustain the necessary temperatures and pressures required for controlled nuclear fusion reactions. Researchers are also exploring ways to minimize the amount of radioactive waste generated by fusion power and to ensure the safety and reliability of fusion reactors.

Despite these challenges, fusion power has the potential to play a key role in the transition to a more sustainable and renewable energy future. As research continues, it is likely that this technology will become increasingly important in the years to come.

Gravity battery

A gravity battery is a type of energy storage system that uses gravity to store and release energy. It works by raising and lowering heavy objects, such as large masses of concrete or steel, in order to store or release potential energy.

The basic principle of a gravity battery is to raise a heavy object to a high position, such as the top of a tower or building, in order to store potential energy. When energy is needed, the object is allowed to fall or descend, converting the potential energy into kinetic energy which can then be harnessed and converted into electricity.

One of the main advantages of a gravity battery is its ability to store large amounts of energy for long periods of time. Unlike other types of energy storage systems, such as batteries or capacitors, which can degrade over time and lose their charge, a gravity battery can store energy indefinitely as long as the heavy object remains in its elevated position.

Another advantage of a gravity battery is its scalability. Gravity batteries can be designed to store a wide range of energy capacities, from small-scale systems that can power homes or businesses, to large-scale systems that can provide energy to entire cities or regions.

Despite these advantages, there are still some challenges that must be overcome in order to make gravity batteries a practical and economically viable technology. One of the main challenges is developing efficient and cost-effective mechanisms for raising and lowering heavy objects, such as advanced cranes or hydraulic systems. Researchers are also exploring ways to integrate gravity batteries into existing energy systems and infrastructure.

Despite these challenges, gravity batteries have the potential to play a key role in the transition to a more sustainable and renewable energy future.

Smart grid

A smart grid is an advanced electricity grid that uses digital technologies to monitor and manage the generation, distribution, and consumption of electricity in a more efficient, reliable, and sustainable way.

In a traditional electricity grid, electricity is generated at power plants and then transmitted over long distances to homes and businesses through a network of power lines. However, this system is often inefficient, unreliable, and vulnerable to outages and other disruptions.

A smart grid, on the other hand, uses digital technologies, such as sensors, communication networks, and advanced analytics, to enable two-way communication and real-time monitoring of the electricity system. This allows the grid to better anticipate and respond to changes in demand and supply, as well as to more effectively integrate renewable energy sources, such as solar and wind power.

One of the main benefits of a smart grid is increased energy efficiency. By providing real-time information on electricity usage, a smart grid allows utilities and consumers to better manage and reduce their energy consumption. This can help to lower energy costs, reduce greenhouse gas emissions, and increase energy security.

Another benefit of a smart grid is increased reliability and resiliency. By monitoring the electricity system in real-time, a smart grid can detect and respond to disruptions, such as power outages, more quickly and efficiently. This can help to minimize the impact of these disruptions and improve overall reliability.

In addition, a smart grid can help to support the integration of renewable energy sources, such as solar and wind power, into the electricity system. By providing real-time information on the availability of these energy sources, a smart grid can help utilities to more effectively manage the supply and demand of electricity and to ensure that renewable energy is used as efficiently as possible.

Despite these benefits, there are still some challenges that must be overcome in order to fully realize the potential of a smart grid. These challenges include developing new standards and protocols for interoperability and cybersecurity, as well as investing in the necessary infrastructure and technologies. Nonetheless, many countries and regions around the world are already making significant progress in deploying smart grid technologies and realizing the benefits of a more advanced and efficient electricity system.

Space-based solar power

Space-based solar power is a proposed technology for generating electricity from the sun using satellites in space. The basic idea is to place large solar panels in orbit around the Earth that can capture the energy of the sun and transmit it back to Earth using microwave or laser beams.

The advantage of space-based solar power is that it can capture more of the sun's energy than solar panels on the Earth's surface, since there is no atmosphere or weather to interfere with the sunlight. In addition, space-based solar power can provide a constant source of energy, since the satellites can orbit the Earth and receive sunlight 24 hours a day.

The main challenge of space-based solar power is the cost of launching and maintaining the satellites. The solar panels would need to be very large to capture enough energy to make the system viable, and launching and maintaining such large structures in space would be very expensive.

There are also concerns about the safety and environmental impact of transmitting energy from space back to Earth using microwave or laser beams. While proponents of space-based solar power argue that the technology can be designed to be safe and environmentally friendly, there are still many unknowns and potential risks that would need to be addressed before the technology could be deployed on a large scale.

Despite these challenges, space-based solar power remains an area of active research and development, with several countries and private companies investing in the technology. If the challenges can be overcome, space-based solar power has the potential to provide a significant source of clean, renewable energy that could help to meet the world's growing energy needs while reducing greenhouse gas emissions and mitigating climate change.

Artificial uterus

An artificial uterus, also known as an artificial womb, is a hypothetical device that could potentially be used to support the growth and development of a fetus outside of the mother's body. The idea behind an artificial uterus is to provide a safe and controlled environment for fetuses that cannot develop normally in the mother's womb due to various medical conditions or complications.

The concept of an artificial uterus has been explored in science fiction for many years, but it is still largely a theoretical idea in the realm of science and medicine. However, there have been some experimental studies using animal models to investigate the feasibility of developing an artificial uterus.

The basic idea behind an artificial uterus is to create a sterile, artificial environment that mimics the conditions of the mother's womb as closely as possible. The fetus would be placed inside a fluid-filled sac that would be connected to a machine that would supply oxygen, nutrients, and other essential substances to support the fetus's growth and development. The artificial uterus would also need to provide a means for waste removal, as well as temperature and pressure regulation to maintain optimal conditions for fetal growth.

While the idea of an artificial uterus may sound promising, there are many technical and ethical challenges that would need to be addressed before it could become a viable medical option. For example, there are concerns about the safety and effectiveness of such a device, as well as the potential psychological and emotional effects on both the mother and the child.

In addition, there are also ethical considerations related to the use of an artificial uterus, such as questions about the personhood and legal status of fetuses grown outside of a mother's body. Nonetheless, research in this area continues, and it is possible that an artificial uterus may one day become a viable medical option for certain cases where traditional pregnancy is not possible or safe.

Neuroprosthetics

Neuroprosthetics is a field of science and engineering that focuses on developing devices or prostheses that can replace or augment the functions of the nervous system. These devices are designed to interface with the nervous system directly, either by electrically stimulating the nerves or by recording signals from the nerves and transmitting them to a computer or other device for processing.

The goal of neuroprosthetics is to improve the quality of life for people with neurological disorders or injuries, such as spinal cord injuries, Parkinson's disease, or stroke. By providing electrical stimulation or recording and interpreting signals from the nervous system, neuroprosthetic devices can help restore lost or impaired functions, such as movement, sensation, or communication.

Self-driving car

A self-driving car, also known as an autonomous car, is a vehicle that is capable of sensing its environment and operating without human input. Self-driving cars use a variety of sensors, including cameras, radar, and lidar, to detect their surroundings and make decisions about how to navigate through them. These cars are typically equipped with advanced computer systems and algorithms that enable them to analyze and process the data from their sensors in real-time.

The development of self-driving cars is driven by the potential benefits they offer, including increased safety, reduced traffic congestion, and improved efficiency. Self-driving cars have the potential to significantly reduce the number of accidents caused by human error, which is currently the leading cause of traffic fatalities. They can also reduce traffic congestion by optimizing the flow of vehicles and reducing the need for parking spaces.

Several companies and research institutions are actively working on developing self-driving cars. Some of the major players in the industry include Tesla, Google, Uber, and Apple. However, there are still significant challenges to overcome before self-driving cars can become a mainstream technology. One of the biggest challenges is ensuring that the cars are safe and reliable, particularly in complex and unpredictable environments such as busy urban areas.

Regulatory and legal issues are also a significant barrier to the widespread adoption of self-driving cars. Many countries and regions have yet to develop clear regulations and laws around the use of autonomous vehicles, which can create uncertainty and hinder investment in the technology.

Despite these challenges, the development of self-driving cars is continuing at a rapid pace, and it is likely that we will see more autonomous vehicles on the roads in the coming years. As the technology matures, self-driving cars have the potential to revolutionize the way we travel and transform the transportation industry.

Maglev train

Maglev, short for magnetic levitation, refers to a type of train that is suspended above the tracks using powerful magnets. Unlike conventional trains that run on wheels and tracks, maglev trains float above the track and are propelled forward by magnetic forces.

Maglev trains can reach very high speeds, up to 375 mph (603 km/h), because they do not experience the same friction and resistance as traditional trains. They also produce less noise and vibration, and are more energy-efficient than conventional trains. Maglev trains are considered to be a very safe mode of transportation, as they do not have any moving parts that can wear out or break.

The technology behind maglev trains has been around for several decades, and several countries have developed and implemented maglev train systems. The first commercial maglev train system was built in Shanghai, China in 2004, and has since expanded to other cities in China, Japan, and South Korea.

Despite their advantages, maglev trains have some significant limitations. One of the biggest challenges is the high cost of building and maintaining the infrastructure required to support the trains. Maglev tracks require a specialized infrastructure that includes powerful electromagnets, specialized power supplies, and advanced control systems. This can make maglev train systems very expensive to build and maintain.

Another limitation of maglev trains is their limited range. Maglev trains are typically designed for short to medium distances and are not well-suited for long-distance travel. This is because the cost of building and maintaining a maglev train system over a long distance can be prohibitively expensive.

Blockchain

Blockchain is a digital ledger technology that allows for secure, decentralized and transparent record-keeping of transactions. A blockchain is essentially a database that is distributed across a network of computers, with each computer storing a copy of the same database. The database consists of a series of blocks, with each block containing a set of transactions.

One of the key features of blockchain is that it is designed to be immutable, meaning that once a transaction is recorded in the blockchain, it cannot be altered or deleted. This is achieved through the use of cryptographic techniques that ensure the integrity of the data stored in the blockchain.

Blockchain was originally developed as the underlying technology behind the cryptocurrency Bitcoin, but it has since been applied to a wide range of industries and use cases. For example, blockchain can be used for secure online voting, supply chain management, identity verification, and more.

One of the main benefits of blockchain is that it eliminates the need for intermediaries such as banks, governments, or other centralized institutions to verify and process transactions. Instead, transactions are verified and processed by the network of computers that make up the blockchain, which makes the process faster, more efficient, and less expensive.

Another benefit of blockchain is that it provides a high level of transparency and accountability. Since every transaction is recorded in the blockchain and can be accessed by anyone on the network, it is very difficult to engage in fraudulent or illegal activities without being detected.

However, blockchain is not without its challenges. One of the main challenges is scalability, as the current technology is limited in terms of the number of transactions that can be processed at any given time. There are also concerns around the energy consumption of blockchain, as the process of verifying transactions requires significant computing power.

Overall, blockchain is a promising technology that has the potential to transform many industries by providing a more secure, transparent, and decentralized way of managing data and transactions.

Robotics

Robotics is a field of technology that involves the design, construction, and operation of robots. Robots are machines that are capable of performing a wide range of tasks automatically or with minimal human intervention. They can be programmed to perform a specific task, operate in a specific environment, or interact with humans in a variety of ways.

Robotics has applications in many different fields, including manufacturing, healthcare, agriculture, and transportation. In manufacturing, robots are used to automate production processes and perform tasks such as welding, painting, and assembly. In healthcare, robots are used to assist with surgeries, deliver medication, and provide physical therapy. In agriculture, robots are used to plant and harvest crops, while in transportation, robots are used to help with warehouse logistics and self-driving vehicles.

One of the key benefits of robotics is increased efficiency and productivity. Robots can work faster and more accurately than humans, which can lead to increased output and reduced costs. They can also perform tasks that are dangerous, repetitive, or unpleasant for humans, such as working in hazardous environments or performing tedious manual labor.

Another benefit of robotics is increased safety. Robots can be designed to work in environments that are dangerous or impossible for humans to access, such as deep sea or outer space. They can also be used to perform tasks that are hazardous for humans, such as working with toxic chemicals or radioactive materials.

However, there are also concerns around the impact of robotics on employment. As robots become more advanced and capable, there is a risk that they could replace human workers in many industries, leading to job loss and economic disruption. There are also ethical considerations around the use of robots, such as ensuring that they are safe and do not cause harm to humans.

Overall, robotics is a rapidly advancing field that has the potential to transform many industries and improve our quality of life. While there are challenges and concerns around the use of robotics, the benefits of increased efficiency, productivity, and safety cannot be ignored.

CRISPR Gene editing

CRISPR (Clustered Regularly Interspaced Short Palindromic Repeats) gene editing is a powerful technique that allows scientists to make precise changes to the DNA of living cells. The CRISPR system is a natural defense mechanism that bacteria use to protect themselves from viral infections. It consists of two components: a guide RNA that can be programmed to target specific sequences of DNA, and an enzyme called Cas9 that can cut the DNA at the targeted site.

Scientists have adapted the CRISPR system for use in gene editing, by designing guide RNAs that target specific genes of interest. The Cas9 enzyme then cuts the DNA at the targeted site, allowing researchers to add, delete, or modify specific genes. This has a wide range of potential applications, including in medicine, agriculture, and biotechnology.

In medicine, CRISPR gene editing has the potential to revolutionize the treatment of genetic diseases. By correcting or modifying the genes responsible for these diseases, it could be possible to cure or alleviate a wide range of conditions, from cystic fibrosis to sickle cell anemia. CRISPR could also be used to create more effective cancer treatments, by modifying the genes of cancer cells to make them more susceptible to existing therapies.

In agriculture, CRISPR gene editing could be used to create crops that are more resistant to disease, pests, and environmental stresses. This could help to increase yields and improve food security, while reducing the need for harmful pesticides and herbicides.

Despite the potential benefits of CRISPR gene editing, there are also ethical and safety concerns. One of the main concerns is the risk of unintended consequences, such as off-target effects or unintended mutations. There is also the possibility that the technology could be used for unethical purposes, such as creating designer babies or enhancing human traits.

Overall, CRISPR gene editing is a powerful tool that has the potential to transform many fields, from medicine to agriculture. While there are concerns around its use, ongoing research and regulation will be important in ensuring that it is used ethically and safely.

Climate Tech

Climate tech refers to a wide range of technologies that are designed to help mitigate or adapt to the impacts of climate change. These technologies can be applied in a variety of fields, from energy and transportation to agriculture and building design. The goal of climate tech is to reduce greenhouse gas emissions, improve energy efficiency, and help communities adapt to the impacts of climate change.

Some examples of climate tech include:

Renewable energy: Technologies such as solar, wind, hydro, and geothermal power can help reduce the use of fossil fuels and decrease greenhouse gas emissions.

Energy storage: Battery and other storage technologies can help to manage the intermittent nature of renewable energy sources, making them more reliable and cost-effective.

Carbon capture and storage: These technologies aim to capture carbon dioxide emissions from power plants and industrial processes, and store them underground or in other ways.

Sustainable agriculture: Technologies such as precision farming, genetic engineering, and vertical farming can help reduce greenhouse gas emissions from agriculture and increase food security.

Building design: Green building materials, energy-efficient lighting, and smart building systems can help to reduce energy consumption in buildings.

Transportation: Electric vehicles, public transportation, and alternative fuels such as hydrogen and biofuels can help to reduce greenhouse gas emissions from transportation.

Overall, climate tech is an important area of focus for addressing the global challenge of climate change. It offers the potential for innovative solutions to help reduce emissions and adapt to a changing climate, while also creating new economic opportunities and driving progress towards a more sustainable future.

Perovskite solar cells

Perovskite solar cells are a new type of solar cell that are made from a material called perovskite, which has a unique crystal structure. Perovskite solar cells have been studied since the early 2000s and have rapidly gained attention in the scientific community due to their potential to be a cheaper and more efficient alternative to traditional silicon solar cells.

Perovskite solar cells have several advantages over traditional silicon solar cells. They are lightweight, flexible, and can be made using low-cost materials and simple manufacturing processes. Additionally, perovskite solar cells can be engineered to absorb a wider range of the solar spectrum, allowing for higher efficiencies and potentially lower costs.

However, there are still several challenges that need to be addressed before perovskite solar cells can be widely adopted. One major challenge is their stability and durability over time, as they are sensitive to moisture and can degrade quickly in the presence of water. Researchers are working on developing strategies to improve the stability and lifespan of perovskite solar cells.

Despite these challenges, perovskite solar cells have already achieved impressive efficiencies in the laboratory, with some devices achieving over 25% efficiency, which is comparable to the best silicon solar cells. This has led to significant interest from the solar industry, with many companies investing in research and development to bring perovskite solar cells to the market.

Internet of Things (IoT)

IoT, or the Internet of Things, refers to the interconnected network of physical objects that can collect and share data with each other and with other digital systems. This network includes a wide range of devices, such as smart home appliances, wearable health monitors, and industrial machinery.

One of the main benefits of IoT is the ability to collect and analyze data in real-time, which can help companies make more informed decisions and optimize their operations. For example, in manufacturing, IoT sensors can monitor equipment and detect potential issues before they lead to downtime or product defects. In healthcare, wearable IoT devices can track patient health data and alert healthcare professionals to any concerning changes.

Another benefit of IoT is increased efficiency and automation. By connecting devices and systems, companies can streamline processes and reduce the need for manual intervention. For example, in logistics, IoT sensors can track shipments in real-time, allowing companies to optimize delivery routes and reduce delivery times.

Overall, IoT has the potential to transform a wide range of industries and enable new business models and revenue streams. However, it also presents new challenges in terms of data privacy and security, as well as the need for specialized skills and expertise to implement and manage these complex systems.

Best Subreddits for Staying Up-to-Date on Emerging Technologies

Reddit is a social media platform where users can submit and vote on content, which is organized into topic-specific forums called subreddits. It can be used to stay up-to-date on emerging technologies by subscribing to relevant subreddits, where users share news, articles, and discussions on the latest developments in science and technology. By engaging with the community and participating in discussions, users can gain insights and knowledge about emerging technologies and their potential impact on society.

There are many subreddits on science and technology topics that can provide useful information on emerging technologies. Here are some of the most popular and active ones:

r/Futurology: This subreddit is dedicated to discussing emerging technologies, scientific discoveries, and future developments that could shape our world.

r/science: This subreddit is a great source for news, research, and discussion on a wide range of scientific topics. Read about the latest advances in astronomy, biology, medicine, physics, social science, and more.

r/technology: This subreddit focuses on news and discussions related to technology, including emerging technologies, gadgets, software, and hardware.

r/artificial: This subreddit is dedicated to discussing artificial intelligence and machine learning, including news, research, and insights.

r/singularity: This subreddit is focused on the concept of singularity, the hypothetical point at which artificial intelligence surpasses human intelligence and technology advances at an unprecedented rate.

r/OurFutureTech: This subreddit is useful for watching videos related to the latest science and technology news, mostly innovations and research.

r/gadgets: This subreddit is all about the latest gadgets, including emerging technologies like smart home devices, wearables, and drones.

r/cybersecurity: This subreddit is focused on cybersecurity news, threats, and best practices.

r/quantumcomputing: This subreddit is dedicated to the discussion of quantum computing, a rapidly advancing field that could revolutionize computing and data processing.

r/robotics: This subreddit is all about robots, including news, research, and discussion on the latest advances in robotic technology.

r/biotech: This subreddit is focused on biotechnology, including genetic engineering, medical research, and biopharmaceuticals.

r/AskScience: This subreddit is dedicated to answering science-related questions from the community, with answers from verified experts in various scientific fields.

r/AskEngineers: This subreddit is similar to r/AskScience, but focuses specifically on engineering-related questions and answers.

r/DataScience: This subreddit is focused on data science and machine learning, including news, research, and discussions on data analysis, statistics, and programming.

r/Space: This subreddit is all about space exploration, astronomy, and related topics, including news, images, and discussion.

r/3Dprinting: This subreddit is all about 3D printing technology, including news, tips, and discussions on the latest 3D printing innovations and applications.

r/energy: This subreddit is focused on energy-related news, research, and discussions, including renewable energy, nuclear power, and energy policy.

Note that some of these subreddits may require some technical knowledge or understanding of the subject matter, so it's a good idea to read the rules and guidelines before posting or commenting.

Best practices for utilizing Emerging Technologies

Utilizing emerging technologies can be a powerful tool for businesses to gain a competitive edge, improve efficiency, and create new business opportunities. Here are some best practices for utilizing emerging technologies:

Identify the right technology: It is important to identify the technology that will solve the problem you are trying to address or will help you achieve your business goals. It is also essential to evaluate the technology's potential impact on your organization, the market, and your customers.

Create a roadmap: Once you have identified the technology, create a roadmap that outlines how you will integrate it into your organization. This roadmap should include timelines, milestones, and key performance indicators (KPIs) to measure progress.

Build a skilled team: You need to build a skilled team that can implement and maintain the technology. This team should have a deep understanding of the technology and its applications in your business.

Pilot projects: Before implementing the technology organization-wide, it is recommended to conduct pilot projects to test the technology's feasibility and effectiveness. This can help you identify potential issues and make necessary adjustments.

Data privacy and security: Emerging technologies often involve collecting and processing large amounts of data. Therefore, it is crucial to prioritize data privacy and security by implementing appropriate measures, such as encryption and access controls.

Continuous evaluation and improvement: Emerging technologies are constantly evolving, and it is essential to continuously evaluate and improve their use in your organization. This includes staying up-to-date with the latest developments in the technology and incorporating customer feedback to improve the technology's user experience.

Collaboration and partnerships: Collaboration with technology providers, industry peers, and academic institutions can help you stay ahead of the curve and identify new opportunities for innovation.

By following these best practices, businesses can successfully integrate emerging technologies into their operations and gain a competitive advantage.

Businesses that successfully utilize Emerging Technologies for revenue generation

There are several companies that effectively implement emerging technologies to generate revenue. Here are a few examples:

Google: In 2015, Google introduced a new machine learning system called RankBrain, which uses AI to help better understand search queries and provide more relevant results.

RankBrain is designed to interpret the meaning behind queries rather than just matching keywords. It uses a neural network to process large amounts of data and identify patterns that are related to the user's query. This allows Google to return more accurate results even for complex queries or those that are not phrased in a traditional manner.

According to Google, RankBrain is now one of the three most important ranking factors for search results. Since its introduction, RankBrain has helped to improve the relevance of search results and reduce the impact of spam and low-quality content.

Overall, Google's use of machine learning and AI in their search algorithm has been a significant driver of their success. By continuously improving the accuracy and relevance of search results, Google has been able to maintain its dominant position in the search engine market and generate significant revenue from advertising.

Amazon Go: Amazon Go is a grocery store that uses a combination of artificial intelligence, computer vision, and sensor technology to create a completely automated shopping experience. Customers can enter the store by scanning a QR code on their phone, pick up items off the shelves, and simply walk out when they're done shopping. The technology automatically detects what they've taken and charges their Amazon account accordingly. By eliminating the need for checkout lines and cashiers, Amazon Go is able to offer a faster, more convenient shopping experience for customers, while also reducing labor costs.

Uber: Uber is a ride-sharing platform that utilizes GPS tracking and mobile app technology to connect riders with drivers. By leveraging emerging technologies, Uber has disrupted the traditional taxi industry and transformed the way people think about transportation. With its user-friendly app and seamless payment system, Uber has made it easier than ever for people to get from point A to point B. In addition, the company has also been able to collect and analyze vast amounts of data on rider behavior, allowing them to optimize their pricing, routes, and driver incentives for maximum profitability.

Airbnb: Airbnb is a home-sharing platform that utilizes a combination of mobile app technology, online booking systems, and data analytics to connect travelers with local hosts who have spare rooms or entire properties to rent out. By leveraging these emerging technologies, Airbnb has disrupted the traditional hotel industry and created a whole new market for short-term rentals. With its user-friendly interface and rating system, Airbnb has been able to build trust between hosts and guests, while also enabling hosts to earn significant income from their spare space.

SpaceX: SpaceX is a private space exploration company founded by Elon Musk that is leveraging emerging technologies to make space travel more affordable and accessible. By developing reusable rockets and spacecraft, SpaceX has been able to drastically reduce the cost of spaceflight, making it possible for governments and private companies alike to launch satellites, conduct research, and even send humans to Mars. Through its innovative approach to space exploration, SpaceX has created new revenue streams and opened up exciting new opportunities for commercial space ventures.

Peloton: Peloton is an at-home fitness company that utilizes a combination of hardware, software, and content to create a highly engaging and personalized workout experience for customers. With its flagship product, the Peloton Bike, users can participate in live or on-demand spin classes from the comfort of their own homes. By leveraging data analytics and machine learning, Peloton is able to tailor its workout recommendations to each individual user, keeping them engaged and motivated over time. Through its subscription-based business model, Peloton has been able to generate significant recurring revenue and establish a loyal customer base.

Domino's Pizza: Domino's Pizza has been at the forefront of using technology to enhance its business. The company launched an AI-powered virtual assistant called "Dom" that can take orders and answer customer queries. It also created a GPS tracking system that allows customers to track their orders in real-time. Additionally, the company has invested heavily in autonomous delivery technology, which it believes will help it reduce delivery times and costs.

Walmart: Walmart has been experimenting with various emerging technologies to improve its business. One notable example is its use of virtual reality (VR) to train employees. The company created a VR simulation that allows employees to experience various scenarios, such as Black Friday shopping, in a safe and controlled environment. Walmart has also been testing the use of drones for inventory management and delivery.

Maersk: Maersk, the world's largest container shipping company, has been using blockchain technology to improve the efficiency and transparency of its supply chain. By creating a blockchain-based platform called TradeLens, Maersk has been able to digitize the entire process of shipping goods, from booking to delivery. This has reduced the time and costs associated with paperwork and manual processes, and has made the entire process more secure and transparent.

Tesla: Tesla has been at the forefront of using emerging technologies to disrupt the automotive industry. The company's electric cars are powered by advanced batteries and use autonomous driving technology to provide a seamless driving experience. Tesla has also been working on various other emerging technologies, such as solar panels and energy storage systems, which it believes will help it create a sustainable energy ecosystem.

Netflix: Netflix has been using machine learning and AI algorithms to personalize its recommendations to users. By analyzing users' viewing history and preferences, the company is able to suggest new shows and movies that they are likely to enjoy. This has helped Netflix increase customer engagement and retention, and has helped it become one of the most popular streaming services in the world.

Resources to learn about Emerging Technologies

Find below some resources that can be useful to learn about emerging technologies.

World Economic Forum: The World Economic Forum's website has a section dedicated to emerging technologies, which covers the latest trends and developments in areas such as artificial intelligence, blockchain, and the Internet of Things.

TechCrunch: TechCrunch is a popular technology news website that covers emerging technologies and startups. It is a great resource to stay up-to-date with the latest news and trends in the tech industry.

Gartner: Gartner is a leading research and advisory company that provides insights and analysis on emerging technologies. Its reports and research papers can be a valuable resource for companies looking to invest in emerging technologies.

MIT Technology Review: MIT Technology Review is a magazine that covers emerging technologies and their impact on business, society, and the environment. It is published by the Massachusetts Institute of Technology and is a trusted source of information for technology enthusiasts and professionals.

QPT Videos: Watch the latest news about new innovations and research related to emerging technologies at YouTube.com/@QPT

Deloitte Insights: Deloitte Insights is a research and analysis website that covers emerging technologies and their impact on businesses. Its reports and articles are a great resource for companies looking to implement emerging technologies in their operations.

Google AI: This website provides information about Google's artificial intelligence (AI) projects, research, and tools. It includes resources for developers, researchers, and anyone interested in learning more about AI.

Google for Startups: This website provides resources and programs for startups, including mentorship, training, and funding opportunities. It also includes resources for businesses that want to use Google's technologies to grow their businesses.

Google Scholar: Google Scholar is a search engine for scholarly literature, including articles, books, conference papers, and theses. It can be a useful resource for researchers and students who want to learn more about emerging technologies and their applications.

Emerging Medical Technologies

The healthcare industry has witnessed significant growth in recent times because of developments happening in various other fields. Irrespective of technological developments, we cannot underestimate the need to follow a proper healthy diet, avoid junk food, perform suitable exercises, maintain a positive mindset, and obtain good sleep to lead a healthy life. And obviously, technology is helping us to follow these things in a better manner. For example, Smartwatches and fitness trackers help us to know the health of our inner organs up to some level which can help us to take some preventive measures to avoid any potential health issues. And various mobile apps are helping to do yoga and meditation. And, even they help to do eye exercises. At the same time over usage of smartphones causes eye issues and posture issues. We have to agree that technology is a double-edged sword that could help us while having the ability to harm us. We need to control and use the technology in appropriate ways.

Advancements happening in other fields push the healthcare industry further. For example, the fast growth of Artificial Intelligence (AI) enabled the discovery of Halicin, a powerful new antibiotic compound that killed many of the world's most problematic disease-causing bacteria, including some strains that are resistant to all known antibiotics. The growth of AI itself is accelerated by recent advancements in computing systems. Soon, the computing power will be increased further with the help of Nanotechnology, Quantum Computing, Neuromorphic computing, and optical computing systems. The chain of developments will lead to fast growth in various fields including the medical field in the coming days.

AI tool ChatGPT was about 72 percent accurate in overall clinical decision-making, from coming up with possible diagnoses to making final diagnoses and care management decisions. An AI System "BioMind" beats Doctors in diagnosing brain tumors.

An artificial intelligence system that can analyze eye scans taken during a routine visit to an optician or eye clinic and identify patients at a high risk of a heart attack.

Technological advancements enable scientists to explore new concepts in healthcare. For example, researchers developed "Inverse vaccine" which shows the potential to treat multiple sclerosis and other autoimmune diseases. Unlike traditional vaccines that stimulate the immune system to recognize and attack harmful invaders, this inverse vaccine works by erasing the immune system's memory of a specific molecule.

Scientists are working on creating robots (e.g Anthrobot) from human cells too as they believe these biological robots can perform therapeutic work without the risk of triggering an immune response or requiring immunosuppressants. In the coming days, they could be used for clearing plaque buildup in the arteries of atherosclerosis patients, repairing spinal cord or retinal nerve damage, recognizing bacteria or cancer cells, or delivering drugs to targeted tissues.

Immunotherapy research is showing the potential to extend the healthy lifespan of humans. They are aiming to target the root causes of chronic diseases rather than just addressing the symptoms.

Miniaturization of electronics allows ingestible sensors, cameras, and other medical devices. For example, Ingestible device detects breathing depression in patients. Even, Ingestible medical devices can be broken down with light. An inflatable pill is embedded with a sensor that continuously tracks the stomach's temperature for up to 30 days. If the pill needs to be removed from the stomach, a patient can drink a solution of calcium that triggers the pill to quickly shrink to its original size and pass safely out of the body. Ingestible "bacteria-on-a-chip" approach combines sensors made from living cells with ultra-low-power electronics that convert the bacterial response into a wireless signal that can be read by a smartphone. An Origami robot can unfold itself from a swallowed capsule and, steered by external magnetic fields, crawl across the stomach wall to remove a swallowed button battery or patch a wound.

Gene Therapy will play a significant role in redefining the healthcare industry shortly. Gene therapy aims to achieve a therapeutic effect by modifying the genes either in a patient's own cells or in eggs or sperm. It can be used to treat a variety of diseases, including cancer, cystic fibrosis, and HIV/AIDS. The Nobel Prize-winning CRISPR Gene-editing technology is expected to significantly speed up gene therapy development and clinical translation as it is simpler, faster, and more precise than previous gene-editing tools. UK has already approved CRISPR gene therapy "Casgevy" to cure sickle-cell disease.

Apart from using CRISPR for treating diseases, scientists are using it to produce a Bull Calf designed to produce 75% Male Offspring.

CRISPR has been used to edit human genes within the body to address a blindness-causing gene mutation. China's Scientist He Jiankui successfully edited the genes of Twins named Lulu and

Nana so that they wouldn't get affected by HIV which causes AIDS, and even their Brains unintentionally enhanced. CRISPR helps alleviate Depression and lowers Cholesterol. Scientists have created Low-Fat Pigs by editing their Genes with CRISPR.

Scientists have developed a gene therapy that was proven in mice to stimulate nerve regrowth across spinal cord injuries and guide nerves to reconnect to their natural targets to restore mobility.

Researchers in Sweden have <u>developed</u> a microscale device for implantation in the eye, which presents new opportunities for cell-based treatment of diabetes and other diseases.

Brain-computer interfaces (BCIs) are systems that can directly record and interpret brain activity, and then use this information to control external devices or software. This has a wide range of potential applications in medicine, like, restoring function to people with paralysis or other neuromuscular disorders, treating neurological disorders such as epilepsy, Parkinson's disease, and Alzheimer's disease, and improving communication for people with locked-in syndrome.

Using a brain-computer interface, a clinical trial participant who lost the ability to speak was able to create text on a computer at rates that approach the speed of regular speech just by thinking of saying the words.

The use of a brain-computer interface augmented with a virtual walking avatar can control gait, suggesting the protocol may help patients recover the ability to walk after stroke, some spinal cord injuries, and certain other gait disabilities.

Clinical research has demonstrated that a brain-to-computer hookup can enable people with paralysis to type via direct brain control at the highest speeds and accuracy levels.

Implanting BCI will become easy as Elon Musk's Neuralink is working on implanting BCI using Robot.

The usage of BCI can increase further as scientists are working on implanting BCI devices without cutting the skull.

3D printing is also contributing significantly to improving healthcare. Scientists in China were able to grow new ears for five children born with an ear defect called microtia. Cartilage-forming cells were taken from the children's ears and used to grow ear-shaped cartilage. The scientists used CT scanning and 3D printing to build a biodegradable scaffold that perfectly matches the 3D structure of the healthy ear of each of 5 children affected with Microtia. The mold was filled in with cartilage cells taken from the children's deformed ears that were further grown in the lab.

Using 3D printing, researchers developed a glucose monitor with much better stability and sensitivity than those manufactured through traditional methods.

Scientists are exploring bioprinting techniques to pursue functional blood vessels.

A research team uses 3D printing and jelly-like materials known as hydrogels to take a step toward 3D-printed tissues and organs.

Engineers have developed a silicone aorta that could offer a promising alternative to heart transplants.

A research team treated an originally damaged human liver in a machine for three days outside of the body and then implanted the recovered organ into a cancer patient. One year later, the patient is doing well.

Nanomedicine is a rapidly growing field with the potential to revolutionize healthcare.
Nanoparticles can be used to deliver drugs directly to diseased cells, which can reduce side effects and improve the efficacy of treatment. They can be used to detect diseases at an early stage, when they are more treatable. Nanoparticles can act as regenerative medicine to deliver stem cells or other therapeutic agents to repair damaged tissues or organs.

Nanomedicine researchers have found a way to tame pancreatic cancer – one of the most aggressive and difficult to treat cancers – by delivering immunotherapy directly into the tumor with a device that is smaller than a grain of rice.

Nanotechnology could change the lives of thousands of people living with cystic fibrosis (CF) as research shows it can improve the effectiveness of the CF antibiotic Tobramycin, increasing its efficacy by up to 100,000-fold.

Nanodroplets and Ultrasound 'Drills' prove effective at tackling tough Blood Clots.

A stamp-sized device can stick to the skin and can provide continuous ultrasound imaging of internal organs for 48 hours.

Researchers have developed a new biodegradable gel that can help to improve the delivery of cells directly into the living heart and could form a new generation of treatments to repair damage caused by a heart attack.

A new type of ultraviolet light that is safe for people took less than five minutes to reduce the level of indoor airborne microbes by more than 98%.

On adult frogs, which are naturally unable to regenerate limbs, the researchers were able to trigger regrowth of a lost leg using a five-drug cocktail applied in a silicone wearable bioreactor dome that seals in the elixir over the stump for just 24 hours.

Groundbreaking pig heart transplant in a human may help patients awaiting donor hearts.

The Kidney Project's implantable bioartificial kidney may help to free kidney disease patients from dialysis machines and transplant waiting lists in the coming days.

An inflatable robotic hand gives amputees real-time tactile control. The smart hand is soft and elastic, weighs about half a pound, and costs a fraction of comparable prosthetics.

Scientists introduced wireless health monitoring patches that use embedded piezoelectric nanogenerators to power themselves with harvested biomechanical energy. It may lead to new autonomous health sensors as well as battery-less wearable electronic devices.

Scientists have developed an injectable gel that can attach to various kinds of soft internal tissues and repair tears resulting from an accident or trauma.

A smartphone-controlled soft brain implant can be recharged wirelessly from outside the body. It enables long-term neural circuit manipulation without the need for periodic disruptive surgeries to replace the battery of the implant.

Specially engineered contact lenses use tears to monitor patient health.

A study found that hyperbaric oxygen treatments (HBOT) in healthy aging adults can stop the aging of blood cells and reverse the aging process.

The use of telemedicine and remote monitoring technologies is rapidly increasing, allowing patients to receive healthcare services remotely. This can be especially beneficial for patients in rural areas or those with chronic conditions requiring regular monitoring. A research team has developed a method that uses the camera on a person's smartphone or computer to take their pulse and respiration signal from a real-time video of their face.

Researchers have developed a way to use smartphone images of a person's eyelids to assess blood hemoglobin levels. The ability to perform one of the most common clinical lab tests without a blood draw could help reduce the need for in-person clinic visits, make it easier to monitor patients who are in critical condition and improve care in low- and middle-income countries where access to testing laboratories is limited.

MIT researchers have developed a way to incorporate electronic sensors into stretchy fabrics, allowing them to create shirts or other garments that could be used to monitor vital signs such as temperature, respiration, and heart rate.

Researchers have developed a platform for self-testing services which is based on artificial intelligence and designed for medical tasks, such as for analyzing diagnostic images.

Irrespective of medical advancements, the scientific world is still struggling to find a cure for many diseases, especially Cancer.

Monetizing the Machine: Your AI Sidekick for Online Riches

Welcome to the future, where robots don't just steal your jobs, they help you create them! In this chapter, we'll delve into the fascinating world of AI writing tools like ChatGPT and Bard, exploring how they can be your secret weapon for generating online income.

Forget the dusty image of robots in factories; these AI whizzes are wordsmiths extraordinaire, churning out content, code, and creative gold at lightning speed. But before you unleash your inner Tony Stark and build a monetization army, let's break down these AI tools and see how they can work for you.

Meet the AI Masterminds:

ChatGPT: This chatty AI is like your brainstorming buddy on steroids. Think of a topic, feed it to ChatGPT, and watch as it coughs up blog posts, poems, scripts, even musical pieces! Its strength lies in its conversational style and creative spark, making it ideal for generating engaging content, product descriptions, or even social media captions.

Bard: Bard, your friendly neighborhood AI from Google, is the research rabbit hole you never knew you needed. It scours the vast web, synthesizes information, and spits out summaries, translations, and insightful answers to your most burning questions. Think of

Bard as your ultimate fact-checker and knowledge curator, ensuring your content is accurate and well-researched.

Monetization Methods:

Now, let's get down to the brass tacks: how can you transform these AI sidekicks into cash machines? Here are a few ideas to get your creative juices flowing:

Blog Boss: Generate blog post ideas, craft outlines, and even write the first draft with ChatGPT's flair. Use Bard to fact-check your content and ensure it's SEO-friendly.

Social Media Maestro: Brainstorm catchy tweets, craft engaging Facebook posts, and even write Instagram captions that captivate your audience. Let AI handle the heavy lifting while you focus on strategy and community engagement.

E-book Alchemist: Got an e-book idea but feeling writer's block? Use ChatGPT to flesh out chapters, generate different writing styles, and even come up with creative chapter titles. Remember, AI is your tool, not your replacement – edit, refine, and add your own unique voice to make it shine.

Content Writing Whiz: Offer your AI-powered content writing skills to businesses and individuals. Help them write website copy, product descriptions, or even blog posts, leveraging AI for speed and efficiency while adding your human touch for quality.

Translation Titan: If you're multilingual, combine your language skills with Bard's translation prowess to offer accurate and fast translation services. Cater to businesses, individuals, or even online platforms.

E-book Empire: Package your AI-generated content into themed e-books or online courses. Teach others how to use ChatGPT and Bard for specific tasks like content creation or social media marketing.

Prompt Mastermind: Create and sell collections of high-quality prompts for specific AI tools, helping others unlock the full potential of these technologies.

AI is a powerful tool, but it's not a magic money-making machine. Use it ethically and responsibly, ensuring transparency and originality in your work. Remember, AI should complement your skills, not replace them. Your creativity, critical thinking, and human touch are still the secret ingredients to success.

Now go forth, and conquer the online world!

Check out the official websites and communities of ChatGPT and Bard for tutorials, tips, and inspiration on how to use these AI tools effectively.

Remember, the key to success is experimentation and creativity. Don't be afraid to try out different methods and see what works best for you. With a little effort and ingenuity, you can turn your AI sidekicks into your ticket to online riches!

Feel free to adapt and expand on these ideas to fit your specific skills and interests. Remember, the future is bright for those who embrace technology and use it to their advantage. So, go forth and conquer the online world with your AI companions by your side!

Free Tools, Big Dreams: Launching Your Online Business with Zero Budget

Starting an online business can feel like scaling Mount Everest in flip-flops – exciting, but daunting. But what if you could conquer the climb with a toolkit of free online tools? Yes, you read that right – free! No credit card required, just your entrepreneurial spirit and a dash of digital know-how.

So, grab your metaphorical crampons and let's explore some incredible, freemium tools to launch your online venture without breaking the bank:

1. Website Building Warriors:

WordPress: Your trusty knight in shining armor, WordPress empowers you to build stunning websites, blogs, and even online stores, all without coding. Choose from thousands of free themes and plugins to customize your digital haven.
Wix: Prefer drag-and-drop simplicity? Wix is your friend! With its intuitive interface and vast library of templates, you can create a professional website in minutes, even if you're a tech newbie.

2. Content Creation Crusaders:

Canva: Unleash your inner graphic designer with Canva's user-friendly platform. Design eye-catching social media graphics, blog post banners, and even presentations – all with zero design experience!
Unsplash & Pexels: Free, high-quality images are vital for any online business. These websites offer a treasure trove of stunning visuals to elevate your content without burning a hole in your pocket.

3. Social Media Saviors:

Hootsuite: Manage all your social media accounts like a pro with Hootsuite's free plan. Schedule posts, track engagement, and analyze your performance – all from one convenient dashboard.
Buffer: Another social media management champion, Buffer offers similar scheduling and analytics features, alongside a handy browser extension for effortless content sharing.

4. Marketing Mercenaries:

Google Analytics: Your free window into the online world, Google Analytics reveals how people interact with your website. Track traffic, understand user behavior, and optimize your content to attract more customers.
Mailchimp: Build your email list and send captivating newsletters with Mailchimp's generous free plan. Engage your audience, promote your products, and grow your business, one email at a time.

5. Customer Care Champions:

Zoho Chat: Connect with your customers instantly with Zoho Chat's free live chat feature. Answer questions, resolve issues, and offer real-time support, all within your website or app.
Help Scout: Manage customer inquiries like a champ with Help Scout's free plan. Organize conversations, track tickets, and provide exceptional service, building loyalty and trust with your customers.

6. Project management: Trello, Asana, Monday.com

7. Cloud storage: Google Drive, Dropbox, OneDrive

8. Document management: Google Docs, Sheets, Slides, Zoho Docs

9. Web conferencing and video calls: Zoom, Google Meet, Skype

10. Image editing: GIMP, Paint.NET

11. PDF editor: Sejda PDF, PDFescape

12. Landing page builders: Unbounce, Leadpages, Instapage

Remember:

Free tools are just the first step. Success comes from dedication, creativity, and consistent effort. Use these tools strategically, learn from online resources, and constantly adapt your approach.

Combine these tools for an even greater impact! For example, use Canva to create social media graphics for Hootsuite scheduling, or leverage Mailchimp's email marketing alongside Google Analytics insights for targeted campaigns.

The online world is your oyster, and with these free tools at your disposal, you're well on your way to launching and scaling your dream online business. So, go forth, conquer the digital frontier, and remember – free doesn't mean cheap, it means limitless potential!

By effectively utilizing these free tools, you can save money, streamline your operations, and boost your small business's success. However, keep in mind that while these tools are listed as free, they may start charging fees at any point and may have limitations in their free versions. Paid versions generally offer more features. Therefore, carefully analyze each tool before you start using it. Consider whether having more control and freedom, even at a low cost, outweighs the advantages of a free service with potential limitations. For example, our Timesheet software offers full source code at a very low price, giving you more freedom and flexibility than any free cloud-based option. With the source code, you can make customizations, avoid surprise price increases, and escape the frequent feature limitations imposed by free services.

Building a Tech Empire: From Startup to Success in the Emerging Tech Landscape

The world of technology is a thrilling frontier, constantly churning out innovations that reshape our lives and industries. In this dynamic landscape, ambitious minds dream of building empires – not of bricks and mortar, but of code and circuits, of ideas that revolutionize the way we live, work, and interact. But how does one navigate the treacherous terrain of startups and emerge victorious, a tech titan at the helm of a thriving empire?

Laying the Foundation: Vision and Validation

It all begins with a spark, a vision of how your emerging technology can solve a problem, improve a process, or simply make the world a better place. This vision isn't just a daydream; it's the bedrock of your empire. Research your target market, validate the need for your solution, and ensure your innovation fills a gap, not just adds to the noise.

Building the Team: Assembling the Avengers of Innovation

No tech empire is built by a lone wolf. You need to assemble a dream team, a diverse group of minds who complement your strengths and fill your weaknesses. Look for individuals with not only technical expertise but also passion, creativity, and a shared vision for your venture. Remember, your team is your family, the ones who will weather the inevitable storms and celebrate the triumphs.

From Prototype to Launch: The Art of Iteration

Your vision is clear, your team is assembled, now it's time to transform your vision into reality. Start with a minimum viable product (MVP), a bare-bones version of your solution that allows you to gather feedback and iterate rapidly. Don't be afraid to pivot, to adapt and refine your offering based on user experience and market demands. Remember, the most successful tech empires are built on a foundation of agility and continuous improvement.

Funding the Future: From Bootstrapping to Unicorns

The road to tech empire is rarely paved with gold. Funding your venture can be a daunting task, but it's not insurmountable. Bootstrap your initial stages, utilizing your own resources and seeking creative funding solutions like angel investors or crowdfunding platforms. As your venture gains traction, explore larger funding options like venture capital, but remember, with each dollar comes responsibility. Choose investors who align with your vision and can provide strategic guidance, not just financial backing.

Marketing the Magic: Spreading the Word of Innovation

Building a tech empire isn't just about building a great product; it's about telling the world about it. Utilize the power of digital marketing to reach your target audience, crafting compelling narratives that showcase the value proposition of your technology. Leverage social media, content marketing, and strategic partnerships to build brand awareness and generate excitement. Remember, in the digital age, your story is your most powerful asset.

Scaling the Summit: From Startup to Global Player

As your venture grows, you'll face the challenge of scaling your operations. Streamline your processes, automate tasks, and build a robust infrastructure that can handle the demands of a growing empire. Embrace the power of cloud computing, data analytics, and artificial intelligence to optimize your operations and gain a competitive edge. Remember, growth is inevitable, but it must be managed strategically to avoid missteps and maintain stability.

The Never-Ending Quest: Innovation and Adaptation

The tech landscape is a constantly evolving beast. To remain atop the empire, you must embrace innovation as a core value. Continuously invest in research and development, explore emerging technologies, and stay ahead of the curve. Be prepared to adapt your vision and strategy as the market demands. Remember, the only constant in tech is change, and those who adapt the fastest will thrive.

Building a tech empire is not for the faint of heart. It demands unwavering passion, relentless dedication, and the ability to navigate uncertainty with grace and resilience. But for those who dare to dream big and translate their vision into reality, the rewards are immense – the satisfaction of creating something truly transformative, the thrill of leading a team of passionate minds, and the legacy of leaving a lasting mark on the world. So, step into the arena of emerging technologies, assemble your team, and embark on your journey to building a tech empire that will stand the test of time.

Remember, the future is yours to shape. Go forth, innovate, and build your empire!

Cutting Through the Hype: Separating Fact from Fiction in the Emerging Tech Buzz

The world of emerging technology is a glittering mirage, shimmering with promises of revolution and reinvention. But amidst the dazzling headlines and breathless pronouncements, lies a treacherous terrain of hype, exaggeration, and downright falsehood. For entrepreneurs, investors, and anyone navigating this exciting yet volatile landscape, the ability to separate fact from fiction is crucial.

So, how do we sift through the hype and identify the genuine game-changers?

1. The Hype Machine: Recognizing Red Flags

- Exaggerated Claims: Be wary of promises that sound too good to be true. Claims like "cure all diseases" or "eliminate poverty overnight" are often red flags. Look for evidence and data to back up the claims, not just flashy presentations and charismatic pitches.
- Tech Mysticism: Jargon-heavy explanations that are intentionally obfuscating the technology's actual workings should raise eyebrows. Remember, true innovation often lies in simplifying complex concepts, not making them more obscure.
- The Bandwagon Effect: Don't get caught up in the herd mentality. Just because everyone's talking about a technology doesn't mean it's worth your time or investment. Do your own research and analysis before joining the bandwagon.

2. Tools of the Discerning Mind: Assessing the Evidence

- Follow the Money: Who stands to gain from the success of this technology? Investors, corporations, and research institutions often have vested interests in promoting certain technologies, so be mindful of potential biases.
- Seek Independent Validation: Look for research papers, peer reviews, and independent analyses of the technology. Don't rely solely on the company's own marketing materials.
- Compare and Contrast: Put the technology in context. How does it compare to existing solutions? What are its limitations and potential drawbacks? A holistic understanding helps separate hype from genuine progress.

3. Beyond the Buzz: Cultivating a Critical Eye

- Develop a healthy dose of skepticism: Question everything you hear and read. Challenge assumptions and don't be afraid to poke holes in the narrative.
- Embrace the power of "wait and see": Not every technology lives up to its initial hype. Give promising innovations time to mature and demonstrate real-world impact before jumping on the bandwagon.
- Stay informed, but not overwhelmed: Keep up with the latest developments in emerging technologies, but don't let the constant buzz distract you from your own critical thinking.

Navigating the world of emerging technology is an exhilarating adventure, but it's one that requires a discerning mind and a healthy dose of skepticism. By recognizing the red flags of hype, utilizing tools of assessment, and cultivating a critical eye, we can ensure that our decisions and investments are based on reality, not the mirage of the tech buzz. Remember, the future is shaped not by the loudest voices, but by those who can see through the noise and identify the true potential of innovation. So, go forth, explore, and let curiosity be your guide, but always remember to keep your critical thinking cap on!

Interesting Innovations

Find below some interesting and useful innovations. While these innovations aren't organized in any particular order, I believe exploring them can offer valuable insights into emerging technologies. You can watch more details about these innovations in my YouTube Channel, or at Jone.Live website.

Graphene quantum dots show promise as novel magnetic field sensors
Physicists found that speeding electrons trapped in circular loops in graphene quantum dots are highly sensitive to external magnetic fields.

Edible electronics: How a seaweed second skin could transform health and fitness sensor tech
Scientists at the University of Sussex have successfully trialed new biodegradable health sensors that could change the way we experience personal healthcare and fitness monitoring technology.

Tiny new climbing robot was inspired by geckos and inchworms
A tiny robot that could one day help doctors perform surgery was inspired by the incredible gripping ability of geckos and the efficient locomotion of inchworms.

Custom, 3D-printed heart replicas look and pump just like the real thing
MIT engineers are hoping to help doctors tailor treatments to patients' specific heart form and function, with a custom robotic heart. The team has developed a procedure to 3D print a soft and flexible replica of a patient's heart.

Wooden Seed Carriers Mimic the Behavior of Self-Burying Seeds
Inspired by Erodium seeds, researchers worked to engineer a biodegradable seed carrier referred to as E-seed which could enable aerial seeding of difficult-to-access areas.

Engineers invent vertical, full-color microscopic LEDs
MIT engineers have developed a new way to make sharper, defect-free displays. Instead of patterning red, green, and blue diodes side by side in a horizontal patchwork, the team has invented a way to stack the diodes to create vertical, multicolored pixels. It will be useful for small displays like smart watches and virtual reality devices to make lively, vivid images.

Targeting cancer with a multidrug nanoparticle
MIT chemists designed a bottlebrush-shaped nanoparticle that can be loaded with multiple drugs, in ratios that can be easily controlled. Using these particles, the researchers were able to calculate and then deliver the optimal ratio of three cancer drugs used to treat multiple myeloma.

New Tool uses Ultrasound 'Tornado' to break down Blood Clots
Researchers have developed a new tool and technique that uses "vortex ultrasound" – a sort of ultrasonic tornado – to break down blood clots in the brain. The new approach worked more quickly than existing techniques to eliminate clots formed in an in vitro model of cerebral venous sinus thrombosis (CVST).

AI Tool for detecting future lung cancer risk
MIT researchers have developed an artificial intelligence tool, named "Sybil" for lung cancer risk assessment. Deep-learning model takes a personalized approach to assessing each patient's risk of lung cancer based on CT scans.

'Living medicine' created to tackle drug-resistant lung infections
Researchers have designed the first 'living medicine' to treat lung infections. The treatment targets Pseudomonas aeruginosa, a type of bacteria which is naturally resistant to many types of antibiotics and is a common source of infections in hospitals.

Printable Sensors Glow when they detect Viruses or other Dangers
Researchers at Tufts School of Engineering have developed a way to detect bacteria, toxins, and dangerous chemicals in the environment using a biopolymer sensor that can be printed like ink on a wide range of materials, including wearable items such as gloves, masks, or everyday clothing.

Deflecting lightning with a laser lightning rod
A European consortium has managed to guide lightning using a high-power laser installed at the top of Mount Säntis in Switzerland.

Turning abandoned mines into batteries
A novel technique called Underground Gravity Energy Storage turns decommissioned mines into long-term energy storage solutions, thereby supporting the sustainable energy transition.

Spray-on smart skin uses AI to rapidly understand hand tasks
A new smart skin developed at Stanford University might foretell a day when people type on invisible keyboards, identify objects by touch alone, or allow users to communicate by hand gestures with

apps in immersive environments.

Aging of Mice reversed

An international study 13 years in the making demonstrates for the first time that degradation in the way DNA is organized and regulated — known as epigenetics — can drive aging in an organism, independently of changes to the genetic code itself. The work shows that a breakdown in epigenetic information causes mice to age and that restoring the integrity of the epigenome reverses those signs of aging.

Artificial nerve cells – almost like biological

Researchers at Linköping University (LiU), Sweden, have created an artificial organic neuron that closely mimics the characteristics of biological nerve cells. This artificial neuron can stimulate natural nerves, making it a promising technology for various medical treatments in the future.

AI Tool VALL-E can imitate anyone's voice with just a three-second sample

Microsoft released an artificial intelligence tool named as VALL-E that can replicate people's voices just by listening 3-seconds audio of their speech

3D Laptop

Asus introduced glasses-free 3D tech with its ProArt Studio 16 laptop. We can switch smoothly between 2D and 3D visualization with one click. Asus is calling this technology spatial vision and it basically relies on eye tracking and lenticular lenses to deliver two separate images to our eye at the same time. We will be able to watch 3D models or even 3D movies without the need for any glasses.

Cheap, sustainable hydrogen through solar power

A new kind of solar panel, developed at the University of Michigan, has achieved 9% efficiency in converting water into hydrogen and oxygen—mimicking a crucial step in natural photosynthesis. Outdoors, it represents a major leap in the technology, nearly 10 times more efficient than solar water-splitting experiments of its kind.

Secret of durable Roman concrete
An unexpected ancient manufacturing strategy may hold the key to designing concrete that lasts for millennia. Researchers found that a calcium-rich lime clast is responsible for the unique self-healing properties of this ancient material.

Hands-free connected home urine lab
Health Technology Company Withings released a new gadget "U-Scan" at CES 2023 in Las Vegas. The U-Scan is designed to be installed in the toilet bowl, which gives users hands-free access to urine analysis.

Flying Car
ASKA A5 is the first viable electric Vertical Takeoff and Landing (eVTOL) vehicle where you can drive on the road like a car and take off vertically to fly in the air like an aircraft.

MoodUP refrigerator
LG's new MoodUP refrigerator lets you customize your space by changing the color of the doors via a few taps on the LG ThinQ app.

Wooden touch interface to improve your Sleep
Emma and mui Lab plan on developing a smart product within the sleep space featuring a wooden touch interface. The interface brings a calm sleep experience to the bedroom and enables people to leave their cellphone outside of a space meant for sleep.

AI technology to upscale old blurry videos on web browser itself
Nvidia's latest AI technology can upscale old blurry videos on web browser itself. Coming to GeForce RTX 40 and 30 Series GPUs next month, the RTX Video Super Resolution feature uses AI to improve the quality of any video watched in a browser by removing blocky compression artifacts and upscaling video resolution.

Morning exposure to deep red light improves declining eyesight
Just three minutes of exposure to deep red light once a week, when

delivered in the morning, can significantly improve declining eyesight, finds a pioneering new study by University College London (UCL) researchers.

Green Light Therapy Shown to Reduce Migraine Frequency, Intensity
New research from the University of Arizona Health Sciences found that people who suffer from migraine may benefit from green light therapy, which was shown to reduce the frequency and intensity of headaches and improve patient quality of life

5-minute breathing workout lowers blood pressure as much as exercise, drugs
New research shows that working out just five minutes daily via a practice described as "strength training for your breathing muscles" lowers blood pressure and improves some measures of vascular health as well as, or even more than, aerobic exercise or medication.

Lanosterol Eye Drops can cure Cataract without Surgery
Researchers in the US have developed a new drug that can be delivered directly into the eye via an eye dropper to shrink down and dissolve cataracts.

Gel sheet to absorb liquid effectively
"Gel sheet" developed by researchers at the University of Maryland can quickly absorb more water than a commercial cloth pad. The sheet swells and holds water without dripping. And, it can quickly soak up more blood without dripping.

Near-Field Ground Projections
Near-Field Ground Projections expand communication and safety features beyond the vehicle.

World's First Truly Wireless TV
Displace TVs solve many of the common problems associated with flat-screen television, which are often unwieldy, tedious to mount to walls and cause damage, cluttered with wires and utilize antiquated remote controls.

Gold-based passive heating for eyewear
Researchers from ETH Zurich have developed a new transparent gold nanocoating that harnesses sunlight to heat the lenses of glasses, thereby preventing them from fogging in humid conditions. This coating could potentially also be applied to car windshields.

'Gelbots' can crawl through human bodies to deliver medicine
A new gelatinous robot that crawls, powered by nothing more than temperature change and clever design, brings "a kind of intelligence" to the field of soft robotics.

Samsung Safety Truck
Samsung has developed an innovative technology using wireless camera and video wall for improving Road Safety.

Wireless 'Skin VR' to provide a vivid, personalized touch experience in the virtual world
A team led by the City University of Hong Kong (CityU) researchers recently developed an advanced wireless haptic interface system, called WeTac, worn on the hand, which has soft, ultrathin features, and collects personalised tactile sensation data to provide a vivid touch experience in the metaverse. The system has application potential in gaming, sports and skills training, social activities, and remote robotic controls.

Producing 'green' energy — literally — from living plant 'bio-solar cells'
Researchers reporting in ACS Applied Materials & Interfaces have, for the first time, used a succulent plant to create a living "bio-solar cell" that runs on photosynthesis

Implantable ventilator
MIT engineers have developed a soft, robotic, and implantable ventilator that is designed to augment the diaphragm's natural contractions.

Paper-thin solar cell
MIT researchers have developed a scalable fabrication technique to produce ultrathin, lightweight solar cells that can be stuck onto any

surface.

Low-cost battery built with four times the capacity of lithium
Researchers are hoping that a new, low-cost battery which holds
four times the energy capacity of lithium-ion batteries and is far
cheaper to produce will significantly reduce the cost of transitioning
to a decarbonised economy.

Free online AI Tool to understand any research paper easily
The AI Assitant Tool SciSpace CoPilot is useful for reading and
understanding research papers easily.

Soft robot detects damage and heals itself
Researchers installed SHeaLDS – self-healing light guides for
dynamic sensing – in a soft robot resembling a four-legged starfish
and equipped with feedback control. After the researchers
punctured one of its legs, the robot was able to detect the damage
and self-heal the cuts.

Fitness levels accurately predicted using wearable devices – no
exercise required
Cambridge researchers have developed a method for measuring
overall fitness accurately on wearable devices – and more robustly
than current consumer smartwatches and fitness monitors –
without the wearer needing to exercise.

Brain-Powered Wheelchair
In one of the first studies of its kind, several people with motor
disabilities were able to operate a wheelchair that translates their
thoughts into movement.

MIT engineers develop a low-cost terahertz camera that works at
room temperature
Researchers at MIT, the University of Minnesota, and Samsung have
developed a new kind of camera that can detect terahertz pulses
rapidly, with high sensitivity, and at room temperature and pressure.
What's more, it can simultaneously capture information about the

orientation, or "polarization," of the waves in real-time, which existing devices cannot.

Can your phone tell if a bridge is in good shape?
MIT researchers find data collected by mobile phones could be used to evaluate the structural integrity of bridges.

Clear window coating could cool buildings without using energy
Researchers report in ACS Energy Letters that they have used advanced computing technology and artificial intelligence to design a transparent window coating that could lower the temperature inside buildings, without expending a single watt of energy.

Battery-free, light-powered pacemaker may improve quality of life for heart disease patients
University of Arizona engineers lead a research team that is developing a new kind of pacemaker, which envelops the heart and uses precise targeting capabilities to bypass pain receptors and reduce patient discomfort.

Students are using AI Tool OpenAI Playground to write essays
Recently many people are getting interested to know about AI Tools like OpenAI Playground. Because recently a Reddit post about it became viral. In that post, a student was saying that he uses OpenAI's playground tool for completing school homework, like writing essays.

Facemask can detect viral exposure from a 10-minute conversation with an infected person
Scientists have created a face mask that can detect common respiratory viruses, including influenza and the coronavirus, in the air in droplets or aerosols. The highly sensitive mask, presented in the journal Matter, can alert the wearers via their mobile devices within 10 minutes if targeted pathogens are present in the surrounding air.

Can a robot laugh with you?
Japanese researchers have designed a shared-laughter AI system that responds to human laughter in order to build a sense of empathy into dialogue.

Painless tattoos that can be self-administered
Researchers at the Georgia Institute of Technology have developed low-cost, painless, and bloodless tattoos that can be self-administered and have many applications, from medical alerts to tracking neutered animals to cosmetics.

Chinese astronauts have successfully grown rice onboard a space station
Chinese astronauts have successfully grown rice seedlings onboard the Tiangong space station and this experiment may yield key insights into how astronauts can cultivate food to support long-term space missions.

Eye Implant made from Pig Skin restores vision to 20 people with diseased corneas
Researchers and entrepreneurs from Sweden have developed an implant made of collagen protein from pig's skin, which resembles the human cornea. In a pilot study, the implant restored vision to 20 people with diseased corneas, most of whom were blind prior to receiving the implant.

Researchers change donor kidney blood type using "molecular scissors"
Researchers at the University of Cambridge have successfully altered the blood type on three deceased donor kidneys in a ground-breaking discovery that could have major implications for kidney patients.

A more environmentally friendly air conditioner
Scientists report a prototype device that could someday replace existing "A/Cs." It's much more environmentally friendly and uses solid refrigerants to efficiently cool a space.

Engineers fabricate a chip-free, wireless electronic "skin"
Wearable sensors are ubiquitous thanks to wireless technology that enables a person's glucose concentrations, blood pressure, heart rate, and activity levels to be transmitted seamlessly from sensor to smartphone for further analysis. Most wireless sensors today communicate via embedded Bluetooth chips that are themselves powered by small batteries. But these conventional chips and power sources will likely be too bulky for next-generation sensors, which are taking on smaller, thinner, more flexible forms. Now MIT engineers have devised a new kind of wearable sensor that communicates wirelessly without requiring onboard chips or batteries. Their design, detailed in the journal Science, opens a path toward chip-free wireless sensors.

The best way to take pills according to science
Researchers examining the mechanics of drug dissolution and the natural anatomy of the stomach found that taking a pill while lying on your right side shortens the time it takes for medicine to be absorbed.

MIT's WalkWise helps older adults stay safe and independent
MIT alumni-founded WalkWise uses a motion-detecting device for walkers to allow family members and care professionals to monitor adults with mobility challenges.

Scientists restore cell, organ function in pigs after death
A team of Yale researchers has developed a technology that can delay the cellular degradation of transplantable organs including the heart, liver, and kidneys for hours after death.

Engineered mattress and pillow system uses heating and cooling to fall asleep faster

Bioengineers at The University of Texas at Austin have developed a unique mattress and pillow system that uses heating and cooling to tell the body it is time to go to sleep.

MIT's stamp-sized ultrasound stickers can see inside the body
MIT engineers designed an adhesive patch that produces ultrasound images of the body. The stamp-sized device sticks to skin and can provide continuous ultrasound imaging of internal organs for 48 hours.

Scientists turn dead spiders into robots
Rice University mechanical engineers are showing how to repurpose deceased spiders as mechanical grippers that can blend into natural environments while picking up objects, like other insects, that outweigh them. An open-access study in the journal Advanced Science outlines the process by which the researchers Preston and Faye Yap harnessed a spider's physiology in a first step toward a novel area of research they call "necrobotics".

Earthgrid's Plasma Boring Robot can dig tunnels 100x faster and up to 98% cheap
U.S startup Earthgrid is developing a plasma boring robot that can dig underground tunnels 100x faster and up to 98% cheaper than existing tech.

Robot dog learns to walk in one hour
Researchers at the Max Planck Institute for Intelligent Systems (MPI-IS) in Stuttgart conducted a research study to find out how animals learn to walk and learn from stumbling. They built a four-legged, dog-sized robot, that helped them figure out the details. After learning to walk in just one hour, the researcher Felix Ruppert 's robot makes good use of its complex leg mechanics. A Bayesian optimization algorithm guides the learning.

World's first "Sand Battery"
The world's first fully working "sand battery" is installed in Finland, to store green power for months at a time.

MIT proposes 'space bubbles' to reverse climate change

Building on the work of Roger Angel, who first proposed using thin reflective films in outer space, researchers from the Massachusetts Institute of Technology (MIT) Senseable City Lab (SCL) produced an innovative solution 'space bubbles' that is easily deployable and fully reversible.

Smart textiles sense how their users are moving

Using a novel fabrication process, MIT researchers have produced smart textiles that snugly conform to the body so they can sense the wearer's posture and motions. By incorporating a special type of plastic yarn and using heat to slightly melt it — a process called thermoforming — the researchers were able to greatly improve the precision of pressure sensors woven into multilayered knit textiles, which they call 3DKnITS.

Giant Swiss 'water battery' can store electricity equivalent to 400,000 electric car batteries

A water battery capable of storing electricity equivalent to 400,000 electric car batteries will begin operating in Switzerland. With the ability to store and generate vast quantities of hydroelectric energy, the battery will play an important role in stabilising power supplies in Switzerland and Europe. A water battery or pumped storage power plant is a type of hydroelectric energy storage. The battery is made from two large pools of water located at different heights.

Wearable muscles

Researchers at ETH Zurich have developed a wearable textile exomuscle that serves as an extra layer of muscles. They aim to use it to increase the upper body strength and endurance of people with restricted mobility.

This Robot paints like a Human

Graduate students at the Georgia Institute of Technology have built the first graffiti-painting robot system that mimics the fluidity of human movement. Aptly named GTGraffiti, the system uses motion capture technology to record human painting motions and then composes and processes the gestures to program a cable-driven robot that spray paints graffiti artwork.

Blood Pressure E-Tattoo Promises Continuous, Mobile Monitoring
Researchers at The University of Texas at Austin and Texas A&M University have developed an electronic tattoo that can be worn comfortably on the wrist for hours and deliver continuous blood pressure measurements at an accuracy level exceeding nearly all available options on the market today.

LEGO-like artificial intelligence chip
MIT engineers have created a reconfigurable AI chip that comprises alternating layers of sensing and processing elements that can communicate with each other.

Injectable gel to repair damage after a heart attack
New gel technology could form a new type of treatment to help hearts regenerate after injury. University of Manchester researchers have developed a new biodegradable gel that can help to improve the delivery of cells directly into the living heart and could form a new generation of treatments to repair damage caused by a heart attack.

Direct sound printing
Most 3D printing methods currently in use rely either on photo (light)- or thermo (heat)-activated reactions to achieve precise manipulation of polymers. The development of a new platform technology called direct sound printing (DSP), which uses soundwaves to produce new objects, may offer a third option.

Tracking sleep with a self-powering smart pillow
People who struggle for shut-eye could benefit from monitoring their sleep, but they have limited options for doing so. In a new study in ACS Applied Materials & Interfaces, one team describes a potential solution: a self-powering smart pillow that tracks the position of the head.

Tiny robotic crab
Northwestern University engineers have developed the smallest-ever remote-controlled walking robot — and it comes in the form of a tiny, adorable peekytoe crab.

Brain death could be reversible, as scientists bring dead eyes back to life
Dead eyes from organ donors have been "brought back to life" in a breakthrough which hints that brain death may be reversible.

Plastic-eating Enzyme could eliminate Billions of Tons of Landfill Waste
An enzyme variant created by engineers and scientists at The University of Texas at Austin can break down environment-throttling plastics that typically take centuries to degrade in just a matter of hours to days.

From seawater to drinking water, with the push of a button
MIT researchers have developed a portable desalination unit, weighing less than 10 kilograms, that can remove particles and salts to generate drinking water. It generates clear, clean drinking water without the need for filters or high-pressure pumps.

Green concrete
In collaboration with researchers at the University of Illinois at Urbana-Champaign, Meta researchers have developed a new AI model that optimizes concrete mixtures for sustainability as well as strength. In early field testing, carbon emission was reduced by 40 percent, while strength requirements were exceeded. Cement in concrete accounts for approximately 8 percent of carbon emissions globally. If successful, the impact of this work could reach well beyond data center construction, as it applies more broadly to the general construction industry.

Paper-thin loudspeaker
MIT researchers have developed an ultrathin loudspeaker that can turn any rigid surface into a high-quality, active audio source. The straightforward fabrication process they introduced can enable the thin-film devices to be produced at scale.

Scientists created Crispier Chocolate using 3D Printers
In research that was published in the journal Soft Matter, researchers from the University of Amsterdam, Delft University, and Unilever, demonstrate that the mouthfeel of an edible

substance can be designed, just like properties of many other materials can.

A new heat engine with no moving parts is as efficient as a steam turbine

Engineers at MIT and the National Renewable Energy Laboratory (NREL) have designed a heat engine with no moving parts. Their new demonstrations show that it converts heat to electricity with over 40 percent efficiency — a performance better than that of traditional steam turbines. The heat engine is a thermophotovoltaic (TPV) cell, similar to a solar panel's photovoltaic cells, that passively captures high-energy photons from a white-hot heat source and converts them into electricity.

AI predicts if and when someone will experience cardiac arrest

A new artificial intelligence-based approach can predict if and when a patient could die of cardiac arrest.

World's first LED lights developed from rice husks

Scientists from Hiroshima university created world's first LED light by using rice husks and chemically obtained products.

A wearable device for enhancing deep sleep

Researchers have developed a wearable device that plays specific sounds to enhance deep sleep. The first clinical study has now shown that the device is effective, but not at the same level of effectiveness for everyone.

Deep learning to enable color vision in the dark

Scientists from the University of Irvine have developed a new system that combines artificial intelligence (AI) with an infrared camera to capture full-color photos even in complete darkness.

A Solar Panel That Generates Electricity At Night

Scientists have developed a new solar panel that can generate electricity at night. Researchers from Stanford University construct a device, which incorporates a thermoelectric generator that harvests electricity from the temperature difference between the PV cell and the ambient surrounding. They achieve 50 mW/m2 nighttime power generation with a clear night sky, with an open-circuit voltage of 100 mV, which is orders of magnitude higher as compared with previous demonstrations.

System helps severely motor-impaired individuals type more quickly and accurately
Researchers at MIT and elsewhere are developing a system that enables severely motor-impaired individuals who communicate using a single switch to do so faster and with more accuracy. Their system is more flexible than many common interfaces, enabling it to be used for tasks like drawing, gaming, or surfing the web.

Reversing hearing loss with regenerative therapy
The biotechnology company Frequency Therapeutics is seeking to reverse hearing loss — not with hearing aids or implants, but with a new kind of regenerative therapy.

Using sound waves to break up kidney stones
An innovative technique called burst wave lithotripsy (BWL) may provide an effective, more accessible alternative for noninvasive treatment of kidney stones, according to initial human studies reported in The Journal of Urology.

World's first distortion-free stretchable micro-LED meta-display technology
For the first time in the world, the Korea Institute of Machinery and Materials (KIMM) research team successfully developed a 3-inch micro-LED meta-display that does not distort the displayed image, even when the display is pulled in a given direction. This was achieved by using the design and manufacturing technology of metamaterials with unique mechanical properties that do not exist in nature.

These solar panels pull in water vapor to grow crops in the desert
Using a unique hydrogel, scientists in Saudi Arabia created a solar-driven system that successfully grows spinach by using water drawn from the air while producing electricity.

New lightweight material is stronger than steel

Using a novel polymerization process, MIT chemical engineers have created a new material that is stronger than steel and as light as plastic, and can be easily manufactured in large quantities. The new material is a two-dimensional polymer that self-assembles into sheets. Such a material could be used as a lightweight, durable coating for car parts or cell phones, or as a building material for bridges or other structures.

Fitbit for the face

Northwestern University engineers have developed a new smart sensor platform for face masks that they are calling a "Fitbit for the face." Dubbed "FaceBit," the lightweight, quarter-sized sensor uses a tiny magnet to attach to any N95, cloth or surgical face mask. Not only can it sense the user's real-time respiration rate, heart rate and mask wear time, it also may be able to replace cumbersome tests by measuring mask fit.

'Super jelly' can survive being run over by a car

Researchers have developed a jelly-like material that can withstand the equivalent of an elephant standing on it, and completely recover to its original shape, even though it's 80% water. The soft-yet-strong material, developed by a team at the University of Cambridge, looks and feels like a squishy jelly, but acts like an ultra-hard, shatterproof glass when compressed, despite its high water content.

Needle-free device for collecting blood samples

Loop Medical's innovative technology offers a needle-free, painless and easy-to-use method for collecting blood samples.

High-speed laser writing method could pack 500 terabytes of data into CD-sized glass disc

Researchers have developed a fast and energy-efficient laser-writing method for producing high-density nanostructures in silica glass. These tiny structures can be used for long-term five-dimensional (5D) optical data storage that is more than 10,000 times denser than Blue-Ray optical disc storage technology.

This Robot can find lost items (e.g Keys, TV remote) even if they are buried under a pile

Researchers at MIT have developed a fully-integrated robotic arm that fuses visual data from a camera and radio frequency (RF) information from an antenna to find and retrieve objects like keys, even when they are buried under a pile and fully out of view. The researchers named it as RFusion. The RFusion prototype relies on RFID tags, which are cheap, battery-less tags that can be stuck to an item and reflect signals sent by an antenna.

When walked on, these wooden floors harvest enough energy to turn on a lightbulb

Researchers from Switzerland are tapping into an unexpected energy source right under our feet: wooden floorings. Their nanogenerator, presented in the journal Matter, enables wood to generate energy from our footfalls. They also improved the wood used in the their nanogenerator with a combination of a silicone coating and embedded nanocrystals, resulting in a device that was 80 times more efficient—enough to power LED lightbulbs and small electronics.

Food generator turns plastic waste and inedible biomass into edible protein

Michigan Technological University's research team aims to convert plastic waste and inedible biomass into edible protein. This groundbreaking research has been awarded the 2021 Future Insight Prize by Merck, a leading science and technology company in Germany.

For the First Time, Optogenetic Therapy Partially Restores Patient's Vision

Using a protein found in algae, a new technology partially restored the sight of a completely blind man. He can now locate, identify and count objects using the treated eye while wearing specialized goggles. Optogenetic therapy, or manipulating proteins and cells with light, is an advanced technology developed in the early 2000s that drove major discoveries about the inner workings of our brains. Yet, while actively researched in experimental animals, functional improvement using this method was never reported in humans—until now. In a paper published in the journal Nature Medicine, scientists from Paris, Pittsburgh and Basel, Switzerland, reported the first-ever case of partial vision recovery in a blind patient after optogenetic therapy. The pioneering study describes the first time a patient has achieved partial functional recovery in any neurodegenerative disease by using optogenetic tools.

The whitest paint will help to fight Climate Change by cooling Homes without AC

In an effort to curb global warming, Purdue University engineers have created the whitest paint yet. Coating buildings with this paint may one day cool them off enough to reduce the need for air conditioning.

Using artificial intelligence to generate 3D holograms in real-time

MIT researchers have developed a way to produce holograms almost instantly. They say the deep learning-based method is so efficient that it could run on a smartphone. The new method called tensor holography could enable the creation of holograms for virtual reality, 3D printing, medical imaging, and more.

Materials move without Motors or Hands

Imagine a rubber band that was capable of snapping itself many times over, or a small robot that could jump up a set of stairs propelled by nothing more than its own energy. Researchers at the University of Massachusetts Amherst have discovered how to make materials that snap and reset themselves, only relying upon energy flow from their environment. The discovery may prove useful for various industries that want to source movement sustainably, from toys to robotics, and is expected to further inform our understanding of how the natural world fuels some types of movement.

Smart Tablecloth Can Find Fruit and Help With Watering the Plants

Researchers have designed a smart fabric that can detect non-metallic objects ranging from avocadoes to credit cards, according to a study from Dartmouth College and Microsoft Research. The fabric, named Capacitivo, senses shifts in electrical charges to identify items of varying shapes and sizes. According to the Researchers, this research has the potential to change the way people interact with computing through everyday soft objects made of fabrics.

Researchers create a robotic camera backpack for insects

In the movie "Ant-Man," the title character can shrink in size and travel by soaring on the back of an insect. Now researchers at the University of Washington have developed a tiny wireless steerable camera that can also ride aboard an insect, giving everyone a chance to see an Ant-Man view of the world. The camera, which streams video to a smartphone at 1 to 5 frames per second, sits on a mechanical arm that can pivot 60 degrees. This allows a viewer to capture a high-resolution, panoramic shot or track a moving object while expending a minimal amount of energy. To demonstrate the versatility of this system, which weighs about 250 milligrams — about one-tenth the weight of a playing card — the team mounted it on top of live beetles and insect-sized robots.

Now metal surfaces can be instant bacteria killers

Bacterial pathogens can live on surfaces for days. What if frequently touched surfaces such as doorknobs could instantly kill them off? Purdue University engineers have created a laser treatment method that could potentially turn any metal surface into a rapid bacteria killer - just by giving the metal's surface a different texture. In a study published in the journal Advanced Materials Interfaces, the researchers demonstrated that this technique allows the surface of copper to immediately kill off superbugs such as MRSA.

Graphene Paint

Umeå researchers show how activated graphene, activated carbons and other hydrophobic carbons can be dispersed in water in a form of micrometer-sized particles. The key agent that helps to make these dispersions last for days is the oxidized form of graphene named graphene oxide. The authors have applied for patent for the method to prepare dispersions.

Innovative mechanical system makes it easy to turn bedridden patients

A mechanical system developed at EPFL's Instant-Lab halves the number of hospital staff needed to turn coma patients and makes the task less physically demanding. It has won the approval of the doctors and nurses who tested the system on dummies.

Physiotherapy could be done at home using virtual reality
Virtual reality could help physiotherapy patients complete their exercises at home successfully thanks to researchers at WMG, University of Warwick, who managed to combine VR technology with 3D motion capture.

Toothpaste tablet to eliminate plastic tubes
Two canadian Entrepreurs have developed innovative toothpaste tablets that remove the need for a tube altogether. This tablet form toothpaste is named as "Change Toothpaste".

Using AI to predict where and when lightning will strike
EPFL researchers have developed a simple and inexpensive system that can predict when lightning will strike to the nearest 10 to 30 minutes, within a 30-kilometer radius. The system uses a combination of standard meteorological data and artificial intelligence.

Scientists successfully use a gel to regrow tooth enamel. It may end Dental Fillings
A Chinese research team has developed a gel that can induce the growth of tooth enamel with a precise maintenance of the original structural complexity within 48 hours. So, the Temporary Dental fillings may soon be a thing of the past.

Nanotechnology turns clothing into self-powered remotes
Purdue University researchers have developed a new fabric innovation that allows wearers to control electronic devices through clothing. This waterproof, breathable and antibacterial self-powered clothing is based on omniphobic triboelectric nanogenerators (RF-TENGs) - which use simple embroidery and fluorinated molecules to embed small electronic components and turn a piece of clothing into a mechanism for powering devices.

MIT's fiber-based artificial muscles can lift 650 times their own weight

MIT researchers have developed Artificial "muscles" which can lift 650 times their own weight, and might be used to control robotic or prosthetic limbs. They were able to produce contracting fibers by imitating the coiling-and-pulling mechanism of plants like cucumber.

Samsung's Deepfake AI can create animated talking head from single image

Machine Learning Reseachers from Samsung in Russia have developed a new Deepfake AI system which will be able to create animated talking Head using very few input photos, even with single photo.

China's CRISPR Twins Lulu and Nana might be Smarter than Others

China's CRISPR Twins might have had their Brains unintentionally enhanced.

This Fabric will automatically Cool or Warm as needed

Researcher from University of Maryland have created a Fabric that can automatically regulate the heat passage so that it can keep the wearer at comfortable temperature at all times irrespective of whether the surrounding is Cool or Hot.

Windowless Planes

Emirates Airline has unveiled a new aircraft that features virtual windows. And, it paves the way for removing all windows from future planes, making them lighter and faster.

Third Arm for Multitasking

For many years Scientists have been working on to use the Signals from the Brain to control the Prothestic limbs. Usually this BMI i-e Brain-machine interface Systems have been developed to allow people with motor paralysis conditions to control assistive robotic devices that replace or recover lost function but not to extend the capabilities of healthy users. Now Researchers in Japan report an experiment in which healthy participants were able to extend their capabilities by using a noninvasive BMI to control a human-like robotic arm and achieve multitasking. Experimental results demonstrate that participants were able to reliably control the robotic arm with the BMI to perform a goal-oriented task while simultaneously using their own arms to do a different task.

Cooking Robot
Bangalore-based startup Mechanical Chef has created a Compact Cooking Robot that is more suitable for Indian Homes.

This 'Cold Tube' can beat the summer heat without relying on air conditioning
The Cold Tube works by absorbing the heat directly emitted by radiation from a person without having to cool the air passing over their skin. This achieves a significant amount of energy savings.

Vertical Walking - Manually powered Elevator uses 10% as much Energy as climbing Stairs
"Vertical Walking" is an experimental prototype designed by a Netherlands company "Rombout Frieling Lab". It uses human power to allow movement between floors of a building with only ten percent of the effort needed to climb stairs and without the need for any external power.

MIT's Computer system transcribes words users "speak silently"
MIT researchers have developed a computer interface that can transcribe words that the user concentrates on verbalizing but does not actually speak aloud.

MIT's Invisible "Second Skin" XPL Cream Makes Wrinkles Disappear
Scientists at MIT, Massachusetts General Hospital, Living Proof, and Olivo Labs have developed a new material that can temporarily protect and tighten skin, and smooth wrinkles. With further development, it could also be used to deliver drugs to help treat skin conditions such as eczema and other types of dermatitis.

Using the 'shadow-effect' to generate electricity
Shadows are often associated with darkness and uncertainty. Now, researchers from National University of Singapore (NUS) are giving shadows a positive spin by demonstrating a way to harness this

common but often overlooked optical effect to generate electricity. This novel concept opens up new approaches in generating green energy under indoor lighting conditions to power electronics.

Charging cellphones with Wi-Fi signals using Graphene
Any device that sends out a Wi-Fi signal also emits terahertz waves. Physicists at MIT have come up with a blueprint for a device they believe would be able to convert ambient terahertz waves into a direct current, a form of electricity that powers many household electronics. Their design takes advantage of the quantum mechanical, or atomic behavior of the carbon material graphene.

Bendable Graphene-Based Supercapacitor charges quickly
Researchers have developed a new bendable supercapacitor made from graphene, which charges quickly and safely stores a record-high level of energy for use over a long period. While at the proof-of-concept stage, it shows enormous potential as a portable power supply in several practical applications including electric vehicles, phones and wearable technology.

Graphene smart textiles developed for heat adaptive clothing
New research on the two-dimensional (2D) material graphene has allowed researchers to create smart adaptive clothing which can lower the body temperature of the wearer in hot climates. A team of scientists from The University of Manchester's National Graphene Institute have created a prototype garment to demonstrate dynamic thermal radiation control within a piece of clothing by utilising the remarkable thermal properties and flexibility of graphene. The development also opens the door to new applications such as, interactive infrared displays and secret infrared communication on textiles.

Harnessing the AI Revolution: How to Level Up Your Online Business

The digital landscape is shifting. Artificial intelligence (AI) is no longer a futuristic concept, it's a transformative force shaping the online world. From personalized recommendations to automated marketing campaigns, AI offers a treasure trove of possibilities for online businesses. But how can you, as an entrepreneur, harness this power and propel your business to new heights?

Here's your guide to leveraging the power of AI for an online business boom:

1. Embrace the Personalization Powerhouse:

AI excels at understanding customer behavior and preferences. Use AI-powered analytics tools to personalize your website and marketing efforts. Recommend relevant products, tailor content, and offer targeted discounts to create a unique and engaging experience for each customer. Imagine a clothing store suggesting outfits based on your browsing history and past purchases – that's the magic of AI personalization!

2. Automate the Mundane, Supercharge the Efficient:

Time is your most valuable asset. Automate repetitive tasks like customer service inquiries, social media scheduling, and email marketing campaigns with AI-powered tools. This frees you to focus on strategy, innovation, and building meaningful connections with your customers. Think of it as having an AI assistant working tirelessly behind the scenes, keeping your business running smoothly.

3. Content Creation Made Easy (and Effective):

Struggling with content creation? AI-powered writing tools can generate engaging blog posts, product descriptions, and even social media captions. While human creativity remains irreplaceable, AI can jumpstart your content calendar and provide valuable insights into audience preferences. Think of it as a brainstorming partner, sparking ideas and helping you craft compelling content that resonates with your audience.

4. Data-Driven Decisions, Every Step of the Way:

AI analyzes data like a pro, uncovering hidden trends and patterns. Use AI-powered analytics platforms to understand customer behavior, track campaign performance, and optimize your marketing strategies for maximum impact. Imagine having access to a crystal ball that reveals the future of your online business – that's the power of data-driven decision making.

5. Customer Service with a Human Touch (Powered by AI):

AI-powered chatbots can provide 24/7 customer support, answering basic questions and resolving common issues. This frees up your human customer service team to handle complex inquiries and build deeper relationships with your customers. Think of it as having a friendly virtual assistant who handles the basic inquiries while you focus on building lasting customer loyalty.

Remember: AI is a powerful tool, not a magic wand. Implementation requires careful planning and integration with your existing business strategies. Start with small, targeted projects, analyze the results, and scale up gradually.

The future of online business is AI-powered, and the time to start is now. Embrace the possibilities, experiment, and watch your business soar to new heights.

How Blockchain Can Be Your Small Business Growth Hack

Blockchain technology, initially associated with cryptocurrencies, offers several practical applications for small businesses beyond just financial transactions. Here are some ways small businesses can leverage blockchain's potential for growth, even in its current state:

1. Enhance Transparency and Trust:

- Supply chain management: Track the provenance of goods to ensure authenticity and ethical sourcing, building trust with customers.
- Loyalty programs: Create tamper-proof loyalty programs on a decentralized platform, fostering customer engagement and brand loyalty.
- Data security: Secure sensitive data (e.g., customer information, contracts) on a distributed ledger, minimizing hacking risks and building data security trust.

2. Streamline Operations and Reduce Costs:

- Smart contracts: Automate agreements and payments, eliminating intermediaries and reducing transaction costs.
- Inventory management: Optimize inventory levels through real-time tracking on a shared ledger, minimizing waste and storage costs.
- Fraud prevention: Reduce fraud risk in financial transactions and contracts through the immutability of blockchain records.

3. Access New Markets and Funding:

- Micropayments: Facilitate micropayments for digital goods or services, opening up new revenue streams for creators and artists.
- Decentralized finance (DeFi): Access alternative financing options like peer-to-peer lending or tokenized assets, potentially bypassing traditional financial institutions.
- Global reach: Connect with customers and partners internationally without barriers or intermediaries, expanding your market reach.

4. Build Brand Engagement and Community:

- NFTs: Create and sell unique digital assets (NFTs) linked to your brand, generating revenue and engaging customers.
- Community ownership: Explore decentralized autonomous organizations (DAOs) to involve your community in decision-making, fostering deeper engagement and brand loyalty.
- Transparency and authenticity: Leverage blockchain's transparency to showcase your values and sustainability practices, building trust and attracting customer loyalty.

However, it's important to consider the current limitations:

- Scalability: Some blockchain networks still face scalability challenges, potentially impacting transaction speed and fees.
- Technical complexity: Setting up and utilizing blockchain solutions might require technical expertise, presenting a learning curve for some businesses.
- Regulatory uncertainty: The regulatory landscape surrounding blockchain is still evolving, creating some uncertainty for businesses.

Despite these limitations, blockchain offers exciting possibilities for small businesses. By carefully considering your needs and utilizing available resources, you can explore innovative ways to leverage this technology and drive growth.

Remember, blockchain is still evolving, so ongoing research and adaptation are crucial. But with its potential to enhance trust, streamline operations, and open new markets, small businesses shouldn't ignore its potential for future success. Though blockchain undeniably has revolutionary potential, currently, many scammers exploit blockchain, cryptocurrencies, and related technologies. Therefore, exercise extreme caution when engaging with them. We can hope this situation improves as blockchain matures and gains wider adoption.

Business Motivational Quotes for Aspiring Entrepreneurs

While it's true that pursuing a business related to emerging technologies can offer many opportunities, it's important to acknowledge that there may also be challenges to overcome. We may face a lot of difficulties when trying to earn money by doing any kind of business. Apart from knowing the technical details and business knowledge, it is important to have a positive attitude. It may be difficult to keep a positive attitude at tough times. I believe reading quotes from great people can help to keep ourselves strong at difficult times. Read below some of the motivational quotes.

In the business world, everyone is paid in two coins: cash and experience. Take the experience first; the cash will come later. – Harold Geneen

Try, try, try, and keep on trying is the rule that must be followed to become an expert in anything. - W. Clement Stone

Entrepreneurship is living a few years of your life like most people won't, so that you can spend the rest of your life like most people can't.

Twenty years from now, you will be more disappointed by the things that you didn't do than by the ones you did do. So throw off the bowlines. Sail away from the safe harbor. Catch the trade winds in your sails. Explore. Dream. Discover. – Mark Twain

You were born to win, but to be a winner, you must plan to win, prepare to win, and expect to win. – Zig Ziglar

You must fall in love with what you do, because being an entrepreneur is a lot of hard work, and overcoming a lot of adversity. From that love will come the dedication that will get you out of bed at 4 a.m. because of a great idea you just had and get you to work till 11 p.m. and not feel tired. – Ken Field

To be successful, you have to have your heart in your business, and your business in your heart. – Thomas Watson, Sr.

Success is not the key to happiness. Happiness is the key to success. If you love what you are doing, you will be successful. – Albert Schweitzer

Success is dependent upon the glands – sweat glands. -Zig Ziglar

Every day I get up and look through the Forbes list of the richest people in America. If I'm not there, I go to work. - Robert Orben

A pessimist sees the difficulty in every opportunity; an optimist sees the opportunity in every difficulty. – Winston Churchill

If you listen to your fears, you will die never knowing what a great person you might have been. – Robert H. Schuller

If there is anything that a man can do well, I say let him do it. Give him a chance. – Abraham Lincoln

The only place success comes before work is in the dictionary. – Vince Lombardi

If I had eight hours to chop down a tree I would spend six hours sharpening my axe. – Abraham Lincoln

Once you say you're going to settle for second, that's what happens to you in life. – John F. Kennedy

Business is more exciting than any game. – Lord Beaverbrook

A man must be big enough to admit his mistakes, smart enough to profit from them, and strong enough to correct them. – John C. Maxwell

Always treat your employees exactly as you want them to treat your best customers. – Stephen R. Covey

In order to succeed, your desire for success should be greater than your fear of failure. – Bill Cosby

Vision without action is daydreaming and action without vision is a nightmare. – Chinese Proverb

The golden rule for every business man is this: "Put yourself in your customer's place". – Orison Swett Marden

Punctuality is one of the cardinal business virtues: always insist on it in your subordinates. - Don Marquis

If the career you have chosen has some unexpected inconvenience, console yourself by reflecting that no career is without them.- Jane Fonda

Time is the scarcest resource and unless it is managed nothing else can be managed. – Peter Drucker

Leadership is a potent combination of strategy and character. But if you must be without one, be without the strategy. – Norman Schwarzkopf

The important thing is not being afraid to take a chance. Remember, the greatest failure is to not try. Once you find something you love to do, be the best at doing it. – Debbi Fields

The winners in life think constantly in terms of I can, I will, and I am. Losers, on the other hand, concentrate their waking thoughts on what they should have or would have done, or what they can't do. – Dennis Waitley

Business is in itself a power. – Garet Garrett

One of the tests of leadership is the ability to recognize a problem before it becomes an emergency. – Arnold H. Glasow

A man should never neglect his family for business. – Walt Disney

The only limits are, as always, those of vision. – James Broughton

If you don't go after what you want, you'll never have it. If you don't ask, the answer is always no. If you don't step forward, you're always in the same place. – Nora Roberts

Your most unhappy customers are your greatest source of learning. – Bill Gates

You can't operate a company by fear, because the way to eliminate fear is to avoid criticism. And the way to avoid criticism is to do nothing. – Steve Ross

Sooner or later, those who win are those who think they can.- Paul Tournier

I don't pay good wages because I have a lot of money; I have a lot of money because I pay good wages. – Robert Bosch

To think that the new economy is over is like somebody in London in 1830 saying the entire industrial revolution is over because some textile manufacturers in Manchester went broke.- Alvin Toffler

I feel that luck is preparation meeting opportunity. – Oprah Winfrey

If you did not look after today's business then you might as well forget about tomorrow. – Isaac Mophatlane

Whether you think you can or whether you think you can't, you're right! – Henry Ford

Who likes not his business, his business likes not him. – William Hazlitt

The man who will use his skill and constructive imagination to see how much he can give for a dollar, instead of how little he can give for a dollar, is bound to succeed. – Henry Ford

If you work just for money, you'll never make it, but if you love what you're doing and you always put the customer first, success will be yours. – Ray Kroc

Being able to touch so many people through my businesses and make money while doing it, is a huge blessing. – Magic Johnson

The entrepreneur always searches for change, responds to it, and exploits it as an opportunity. – Peter F. Drucker

Business is a combination of war and sport. – Andre Maurois

The great accomplishments of man have resulted from the transmission of ideas of enthusiasm. – Thomas J. Watson

Look well to this day. Yesterday is but a dream and tomorrow is only a vision. But today well lived makes every yesterday a dream of happiness and every tomorrow a vision of hope. Look well therefore to this day. – Francis Gray

Surviving a failure gives you more self-confidence. Failures are great learning tools, but they must be kept to a minimum. – Jeffrey Immelt

Whatever the mind of man can conceive and believe, it can achieve. Thoughts are things! And powerful things at that, when mixed with definiteness of purpose, and burning desire, can be translated into riches. – Napoleon Hill

It is not the strongest of the species that survive, nor the most intelligent, but the one most responsive to change. – Charles Darwin.

The only way around is through. – Robert Frost

If you owe the bank $100 that's your problem. If you owe the bank $100 million, that's the bank's problem. – J. Paul Getty

Disneyland is a work of love. We didn't go into Disneyland just with the idea of making money. – Walt Disney

You only have to do a very few things right in your life so long as you don't do too many things wrong. – Warren Buffett

You need to be aware of what others are doing, applaud their efforts, acknowledge their successes, and encourage them in their pursuits. When we all help one another, everybody wins. – Jim Stovall

It takes more than capital to swing business. You've got to have the A. I. D. degree to get by – Advertising, Initiative, and Dynamics. – Isaac Asimov

People are definitely a company's greatest asset. It doesn't make any difference whether the product is cars or cosmetics. A company is only as good as the people it keeps. – Mary Kay Ash

In business, I've discovered that my purpose is to do my best to my utmost ability every day. That's my standard. I learned early in my life that I had high standards. – Donald Trump

The absolute fundamental aim is to make money out of satisfying customers. – John Egan

Let's be honest. There's not a business anywhere that is without problems. Business is complicated and imperfect. Every business everywhere is staffed with imperfect human beings and exists by providing a product or service to other imperfect human beings. – Bob Parsons

The man who does not work for the love of work but only for money is not likely to neither make money nor find much fun in life. – Charles M. Schwab

Far and away the best prize that life offers is the chance to work hard at work worth doing. – Theodore Roosevelt

To win without risk is to triumph without glory. – Pierre Corneille

Management is nothing more than motivating other people. – Le Iacocca

To succeed… You need to find something to hold on to, something to motivate you, something to inspire you. – Tony Dorsett

Whether it's Google or Apple or free software, we've got some fantastic competitors and it keeps us on our toes. – Bill Gates

I have not failed. I've just found 10,000 ways that won't work. - Thomas A. Edison

Effort only fully releases its reward after a person refuses to quit. -Napoleon Hill

Empty pockets never held anyone back. Only empty heads and empty hearts can do that. – Norman Vincent Peale

If you don't see yourself as a winner, then you cannot perform as a winner. – Zig Ziglar

There are no secrets to success. It is the result of preparation, hard work, and learning from failure. – Colin Powell

There is only one boss. The customer. And he can fire everybody in the company from the chairman on down, simply by spending his money somewhere else. - Sam Walton

A goal properly set is halfway reached. – Zig Ziglar

Failure doesn't mean you are a failure it just means you haven't succeeded yet. – Robert H. Schuller

The best executive is the one who has sense enough to pick good men to do what he wants done, and self-restraint to keep from meddling with them while they do it. – Theodore Roosevelt

Positive thinking will let you do everything better than negative thinking will. – Zig Ziglar

The true entrepreneur is a doer, not a dreamer.

Never, never, never give up. – Winston Churchill

How Small Businesses Can Thrive with Emerging Technologies

Boost Efficiency and Productivity:

Automate repetitive tasks: Use AI-powered tools for scheduling, customer service, email marketing, and data entry. This frees up your time for more strategic tasks.

Improve data analysis: Utilize analytics platforms to understand customer behavior, track campaign performance, and optimize your operations. Data-driven decision making can lead to significant improvements.

Embrace cloud-based tools: Migrate to cloud-based software and services for data security, accessibility, and cost-effectiveness. You can access your business tools from anywhere, anytime.

Optimize collaboration: Use digital collaboration tools like video conferencing, project management platforms, and instant messaging to improve communication and teamwork, especially in a remote-first world.

Enhance Customer Experience:

Personalize your marketing: Employ AI-powered tools to deliver personalized recommendations, targeted offers, and relevant content to your customers, creating a more engaging experience.

Offer chatbots for 24/7 support: Implement AI-powered chatbots to answer basic questions, resolve common issues, and provide immediate customer service, even outside business hours.

Leverage social media effectively: Use social media platforms to connect with your customers, create brand awareness, and conduct marketing campaigns. Analyze audience engagement to tailor your content and strategies.

Explore AR/VR technology: Consider using Augmented Reality (AR) for product demonstrations, virtual tours, or interactive experiences, and Virtual Reality (VR) for training simulations or immersive marketing campaigns.

Innovate and Stay Ahead:

Keep up with trends: Attend industry events, read relevant publications, and stay informed about the latest emerging technologies. This will help you identify potential opportunities and adapt your business strategies accordingly.

Experiment with new tools: Don't be afraid to try out new technologies, even on a small scale. Experiment with AI-powered writing tools, design software, or marketing automation platforms to see what works for your business.

Partner with tech startups: Collaborate with young tech companies to access innovative solutions and leverage their expertise. This can give your business a competitive edge and access to cutting-edge technology.

Invest in upskilling: Encourage your employees to learn new skills related to emerging technologies. This will make your team more adaptable to change and boost your overall technological fluency.

Remember:

Start small and scale gradually: Don't try to implement everything at once. Begin with small, achievable projects and scale up as you gain experience and comfort.

Focus on value, not just technology: Technology should be a tool to improve your business, not an end in itself. Ensure that your technology choices align with your overall business goals and create tangible value for your customers.

Be mindful of the cost: Carefully evaluate the cost-benefit of each technology before investing. Choose solutions that provide a good return on your investment and don't overspend on unnecessary bells and whistles.

By leveraging emerging technologies strategically, you can streamline your operations, enhance customer experience, and stay ahead of the curve in your industry. Don't be afraid to experiment, learn, and adapt, and you'll be well on your way to running a successful and innovative small business.

Exploring the Untapped Potential of Nanotechnology

Nanotechnology, the manipulation of matter at the atomic and molecular level, offers a treasure trove of potential business opportunities across various industries. Here's a glimpse into some exciting possibilities:

Healthcare:

- Targeted drug delivery: Nanoparticles can be designed to selectively target diseased cells, reducing side effects and improving treatment efficacy. Imagine cancer medication specifically attacking tumors while leaving healthy tissues untouched.
- Precision diagnostics: Nanosensors can detect biomarkers for diseases with unprecedented accuracy, enabling early diagnosis and personalized medicine. Think of a simple blood test identifying early signs of Alzheimer's before symptoms even appear.
- Regenerative medicine: Growing new tissues and organs is becoming a reality with nanotech-based scaffolds and biomaterials. Picture 3D-printed limbs or even hearts, revolutionizing organ transplantation.

Energy:

- Efficient solar cells: Nanostructured materials can boost the efficiency of solar panels, paving the way for cleaner and more affordable energy. Imagine capturing more sunlight in smaller panels, powering entire cities sustainably.
- Next-generation batteries: Lithium-ion batteries could be supercharged with nanomaterials, offering longer range for electric vehicles and grid-level energy storage. Picture

driving across the country on a single charge or storing
renewable energy for days during peak demand.

- Hydrogen fuel cells: Nanoparticles can optimize hydrogen
  production and fuel cell performance, unlocking the
  potential of this clean energy source. Think of
  hydrogen-powered planes and ships, drastically reducing
  carbon emissions in transportation.

Sustainability:

- Water purification: Nanoscale membranes can effectively
  filter contaminants from water, providing clean drinking
  water even in resource-scarce regions. Imagine turning
  polluted rivers into safe sources of hydration for millions.
- Pollution control: Nanoparticles can capture and neutralize
  pollutants in air and water, combating environmental
  degradation. Picture smog-free cities and healthy rivers
  teeming with life.
- Biodegradable materials: Nanoscale engineering can create
  durable yet biodegradable materials, reducing plastic waste
  and pollution. Imagine packaging that dissolves harmlessly
  after use, leaving no trace in the environment.

These are just a few examples, and the potential of nanotechnology
is constantly evolving. With further research and development, we
can expect even more groundbreaking applications that will impact
every aspect of our lives.

Remember: Entering the nanotech field requires careful
consideration of technical challenges, regulatory hurdles, and ethical
concerns. However, for those with vision and perseverance, the
rewards of harnessing this powerful technology can be immense.

While the cutting edge of nanotechnology might involve million-dollar labs and years of research, there are still ways for individuals with limited resources to tap into the potential of this revolution and generate income. Here are a few ideas:

1. Content Creation and Education:

- Blogging and Vlogging: Share your knowledge and enthusiasm for nanotechnology with the world through blogs, YouTube channels, or social media. Focus on making complex topics accessible to a general audience and build a community of engaged followers. You can monetize your content through advertising, sponsorships, or even online courses.
- Freelance Writing and Editing: Offer your writing and editing skills to companies or individuals working in the nanotechnology field. You can write articles, blog posts, website copy, or even edit research papers and technical documents. Platforms like Upwork or Fiverr can help you connect with potential clients.

2. Consulting and Advisory Services:

- Market Research and Analysis: If you have a knack for research and analysis, you can offer your services to companies looking to enter the nanotechnology market. Conduct market research, analyze trends, and provide valuable insights to help them make informed decisions.
- Technical Consulting: If you have a technical background in science or engineering, you can offer consulting services to nanotechnology startups or research labs. Your expertise can be invaluable in areas like materials science, device fabrication, or process optimization.

3. Skills Development and Training:

- Online Courses and Workshops: Teach others about nanotechnology! Develop online courses or workshops that cover the basics of nanotechnology, its applications in various industries, or even specific skills like nanomaterial synthesis or characterization. You can sell your courses on platforms like Udemy or Skillshare.
- Private Tutoring and Mentoring: Offer your expertise to students or individuals interested in learning more about nanotechnology. Provide one-on-one tutoring sessions or mentorship programs to help them develop their skills and knowledge.

4. Leverage Existing Platforms:

- Affiliate Marketing: Promote nanotechnology-related products or services through affiliate marketing programs. Earn commissions for every sale you generate by referring customers through your blog, social media, or other online channels.
- Participate in Innovation Challenges and Competitions: Many organizations and companies hold innovation challenges and competitions focused on nanotechnology solutions. These can be a great way to gain recognition for your ideas, win prize money, and even attract potential investors.

Remember, success in any field requires hard work, dedication, and continuous learning. Stay updated on the latest advancements in nanotechnology, network with people in the field, and be persistent in your efforts. With the right approach, even limited resources can be the launchpad for exciting opportunities in the world of nanotechnology.

Additional Tips:

- Focus on a specific niche: Nanotechnology is a vast field. Choose a specific area of interest or application where you can develop deep expertise and offer valuable insights.
- Build a strong online presence: Create a professional website or social media profiles to showcase your skills and experience. This will help you connect with potential clients and collaborators.
- Collaborate with others: Partner with other individuals or organizations working in the nanotechnology space. This can expand your reach, access new resources, and open up new opportunities.

By following these tips and leveraging your creativity and resourcefulness, you can turn the nanotechnology revolution into a springboard for your own success.

How emerging technologies are transforming the construction industry

The construction industry, long known for its gritty, hands-on approach, is experiencing a thrilling makeover powered by exciting new technologies. From tiny sensors in your concrete to robots laying bricks and AI optimizing every step, these innovations are paving the way for a safer, more efficient, and sustainable future for builders. Let's delve into some specific ways this transformation is unfolding:

Precision and Efficiency:

- Building Information Modeling (BIM): Imagine a 3D digital twin of your entire project, complete with every piece of material, pipe, and wire in its virtual place. BIM allows planners and contractors to visualize, simulate, and optimize every stage of construction, minimizing errors, boosting efficiency, and catching potential issues before they arise on the real site.

- Drones and Robotics: Picture these buzzing insects not delivering packages, but surveying complex sites, mapping terrain, and performing dangerous tasks like inspecting wind turbines or high-rise facades. Drones and robots are transforming construction by automating tedious tasks, improving safety, and collecting valuable data for better decision-making.

- 3D Printing: Forget traditional bricklaying; imagine printing entire walls or intricate building components on-site. 3D printing is revolutionizing construction by reducing waste, speeding up construction times, and even allowing for custom-designed elements and complex geometries.

Safety and Risk Management:

- Wearable sensors and technology: Imagine construction workers sporting smart vests that monitor vital signs, fatigue levels, and even detect potential hazards like falling objects or proximity to dangerous equipment. These wearable sensors are enhancing safety, preventing accidents, and promoting worker well-being.

- Predictive maintenance and AI-powered safety monitoring: Forget playing whack-a-mole with equipment breakdowns. AI-powered platforms can analyze sensor data from machinery and structures, predicting potential failures and scheduling preventive maintenance before things go wrong. This prevents costly downtime and keeps everyone safe on site.

- Virtual Reality (VR) training and simulations: Want to train construction workers without risking real injuries? VR simulations can immerse trainees in realistic construction scenarios, teaching them safe practices, proper equipment handling, and emergency procedures in a controlled environment.

Sustainability and Environmental Impact:

- Building materials and renewable energy integration: Imagine buildings made from recycled materials, employing solar panels and wind turbines for energy, and even capturing rainwater for reuse. Construction is embracing sustainable practices, reducing its environmental footprint and creating energy-efficient structures.
- Carbon footprint tracking and optimization: Tools are emerging to track the carbon footprint of building materials and construction processes, allowing companies to identify and minimize their environmental impact. This promotes transparency and incentivizes responsible building practices.
- Smart waste management and resource optimization: Innovative systems are streamlining waste disposal on construction sites, sorting materials for recycling, and even repurposing scrap into new building materials. This reduces environmental burden and promotes a circular economy within the industry.

Challenges and Considerations:

- Technology adoption and cost barriers: Not all companies have the resources or expertise to embrace these new technologies readily. Government initiatives and accessible training programs can bridge this gap and incentivize wider adoption.
- Data privacy and cybersecurity: As construction sites become increasingly interconnected and collect vast amounts of data, robust cybersecurity measures and transparent data privacy policies are crucial.
- Ethical considerations and workforce challenges: Automation and AI adoption must be carefully managed to

avoid job displacement and ensure equitable opportunities for all workers. Training and reskilling programs can help the workforce adapt to the changing landscape.

- Standardization and interoperability: Different technological solutions from various vendors can lead to compatibility issues. Industry-wide standards and open platforms can create a more seamless and collaborative ecosystem.

By embracing these emerging technologies thoughtfully and responsibly, the construction industry can build a brighter future. Imagine safer, more efficient, and sustainable projects that not only stand the test of time but also benefit the environment and the communities they serve.

Leveraging Emerging Technologies for Web Developers

The world of web development is constantly evolving, driven by a wave of exciting emerging technologies. As a web developer, staying ahead of the curve and leveraging these tools to your advantage can unlock a treasure trove of benefits, both for your personal and professional growth. Here are some ways you can do that:

Boost your skillset and marketability:

- Embrace Artificial Intelligence (AI) and Machine Learning (ML): Explore libraries and frameworks like TensorFlow or PyTorch to add AI features to your websites, such as personalized recommendations, chatbots, or image recognition. Mastering these skills will make you a valuable asset in the job market.
- Dive into WebAssembly (WASM): This technology allows you to run high-performance code written in languages like C/C++ directly in the browser, opening doors for more immersive and interactive web experiences.

- Get comfortable with serverless computing: Platforms like AWS Lambda or Google Cloud Functions allow you to write and deploy code without managing servers, simplifying development and scaling your applications.

Enhance user experience and engagement:

- Craft progressive web apps (PWAs): These offer app-like features and offline functionality, leading to improved user engagement and accessibility across devices.
- Utilize augmented reality (AR) and virtual reality (VR): These technologies can revolutionize website interactions, creating immersive experiences like virtual tours or product demonstrations.
- Implement voice-based interfaces: As voice assistants become more prevalent, integrating voice commands into your websites can provide a smooth and accessible user experience.

Improve efficiency and optimize workflow:

- Automate repetitive tasks: Tools like Selenium or Puppeteer can automate testing, deployment, and other tedious tasks, freeing up your time for more creative endeavors.
- Leverage code editors with advanced features: Consider editors like VS Code or Sublime Text with plugins for code completion, linting, and debugging, boosting your productivity and code quality.
- Embrace continuous integration and continuous delivery (CI/CD): Automate your build, test, and deployment processes with tools like Jenkins or GitLab CI/CD to ensure faster and more reliable development cycles.

Remember:

- Start small and experiment: Don't try to adopt everything at once. Choose a few technologies that align with your interests and projects, and start experimenting with them.
- Stay updated and keep learning: The tech landscape is constantly changing. Read blogs, attend conferences, and participate in online communities to stay ahead of the curve and acquire new skills.
- Network with other developers: Connect with other developers who are exploring these technologies. Share your experiences, learn from each other, and collaborate on projects.

How Innovative Technologies are Transforming the Teaching Landscape

Teachers are facing a rapidly evolving educational landscape, with emerging technologies constantly popping up and promising new ways to engage and empower students. But how can educators navigate this tech tidal wave and actually utilize it to enhance their classroom practices? Here are some exciting ways teachers can leverage emerging technologies for better learning:

Enhancing Engagement and Interaction:

- Virtual Reality (VR) and Augmented Reality (AR): Take students on virtual field trips to ancient Rome, dissect a virtual frog in biology class, or overlay historical figures onto everyday objects in AR, blurring the lines between classroom and immersive experiences.

- Gamification: Design educational games that make learning fun and interactive. Gamification can cover any subject, from math drills to vocabulary practice, with engaging challenges and rewards motivating students to master concepts.
- Interactive Whiteboards and Collaborative Tools: These digital canvases foster collaboration and active learning. Students can brainstorm ideas, annotate documents, and work on projects together in real-time, promoting communication and teamwork.

Personalizing Learning and Assessment:

- Adaptive Learning Platforms: These platforms assess individual student strengths and weaknesses, dynamically adjusting content and learning paths to fit each student's needs. This personalized approach helps cater to diverse learning styles and ensures that everyone progresses at their own pace.
- Artificial Intelligence (AI)-powered Chatbots: Imagine an AI companion that answers students' questions, provides feedback on assignments, and offers personalized learning recommendations. These chatbots can offer 24/7 support and personalized guidance, extending learning beyond the classroom walls.
- Digital Portfolios and e-Assessments: Instead of traditional tests, students can showcase their learning through digital portfolios that compile projects, presentations, and creative pieces. These e-portfolios provide a holistic view of student progress and allow for more authentic assessment methods.

Promoting Creativity and Critical Thinking:

- 3D Printing and Robotics: Bring STEM concepts to life through 3D printing projects or building and programming robots. These hands-on activities spark curiosity, encourage problem-solving, and teach valuable skills in technology and engineering.
- Coding and App Development: Introduce students to programming languages and empower them to create their own digital solutions. Coding empowers creativity, logical thinking, and problem-solving, equipping students with future-proof skills.
- Blogging and Podcasting: Let students voice their ideas and engage in critical thinking through online platforms. Blogging and podcasting encourage research, analysis, and communication skills, while fostering a sense of community and digital citizenship.

Remember:

- Technology is a tool, not a substitute: Emerging technologies should complement, not replace, traditional teaching methods. The focus should remain on effective pedagogy and meaningful learning experiences, with technology serving as an amplifier.
- Professional development is key: Teachers need to embrace continuous learning and explore new technologies themselves. Workshops, online resources, and collaboration with tech-savvy colleagues can help educators acquire the skills and confidence to implement these tools effectively.
- Equity and access matter: Not all students have equal access to technology. It's crucial for educators to consider accessibility concerns and find creative ways to ensure all students can benefit from emerging technologies, regardless of their background or resources.

By embracing emerging technologies thoughtfully and strategically, teachers can transform the classroom into a dynamic and engaging environment where learning becomes relevant, personalized, and ultimately, unforgettable. So, keep exploring, keep learning, and keep unleashing the power of technology to inspire the next generation of innovators and critical thinkers!

Leverage the 3D printing revolution to earn money on a budget

While owning a 3D printer opens up a wider range of income-generating possibilities, it's not the only path to profiting from the 3D printing revolution. Even with limited resources, you can leverage your creativity and resourcefulness to unlock exciting opportunities in this booming field. Here are some ideas:

Design and Sell 3D Printable Models:

- Focus on a niche: Don't compete with mass-produced items. Find a niche audience with specific needs, like tabletop gaming miniatures, custom phone cases, or personalized decorations.
- Start simple: Begin with affordable 3D modeling software like Tinkercad or Blender. Design practical or playful objects that are easy to print and don't require complex supports.
- Sell your designs online: Platforms like Etsy, Shapeways, or Cults3D allow you to upload your designs for sale. Focus on high-quality photos, clear descriptions, and competitive pricing.
- Offer customization options: Provide options for personalization, like initials, names, or custom colors. This

increases customer engagement and expands your potential market.

Become a 3D Printing Service:

- Partner with local businesses: Offer printing services to makerspaces, artists, or small businesses requiring prototyping or small-batch production.
- Promote your services online: Advertise on social media, community forums, or local classifieds. Highlight your printing capabilities, materials offered, and competitive rates.
- Collaborate with designers: Team up with local designers to offer a print-and-design package. This provides a complete solution for customers and expands your service offerings.

Use Existing Platforms:

- Affiliate marketing: Promote 3D printers, filaments, or other printing-related products through affiliate programs. Earn commissions for every sale generated through your referrals.
- Content creation: Share your knowledge and passion for 3D printing through blogs, Youtube channels, or online tutorials. Monetize your content through advertising, sponsorships, or online courses.
- 3D printing contests and challenges: Participate in online competitions to showcase your skills and win prizes. This can gain you recognition and potential clients.

Remember:

- Focus on quality and customer service: Deliver high-quality prints and reliable service to build trust and repeat business.
- Stay updated on trends: Keep up with the latest advancements in 3D printing technology and materials to offer innovative solutions to your customers.
- Network and build relationships: Connect with other 3D printing enthusiasts, professionals, and potential customers. Collaboration can open new doors and opportunities.

With dedication, creativity, and resourcefulness, you can carve your own path to success in the 3D printing revolution. Don't let limited resources deter you; remember, the most valuable assets are your imagination and your drive to learn and grow.

How Telemedicine is Transforming Patient Care

Telemedicine, also known as telehealth, encompasses the delivery of healthcare services remotely using information and communication technologies. It allows doctors, nurses, and other healthcare professionals to connect with patients virtually, across geographic and temporal barriers. This can be through:

Real-time interactions:

- Video consultations: Video conferencing platforms enable face-to-face consultations, remote physical examinations, and real-time discussions of symptoms and concerns.
- Remote monitoring: Wearable devices and sensors can track vital signs like heart rate, blood pressure, and oxygen levels, providing doctors with continuous data and allowing for proactive interventions.

- Phone consultations: Simple phone calls remain a valuable tool for quick consultations, follow-up appointments, and medication management.

Store-and-forward interactions:

- Asynchronous messaging: Platforms allow patients to submit medical information, photos, and questions via text or video messages, which healthcare professionals can review and respond to at their convenience.
- Telediagnosis and e-prescriptions: Doctors can analyze medical images and data remotely, even from different locations, and send prescriptions electronically to pharmacies.
- Online consultations and support groups: Virtual platforms offer access to specialists, therapists, and support groups, overcoming geographical limitations and improving accessibility for patients in rural areas or with mobility issues.

Benefits of Telemedicine:

- Improved access to healthcare: Telemedicine eliminates geographic and transportation barriers, providing care to patients in remote areas or with limited mobility.
- Increased patient convenience: Virtual consultations reduce waiting times, travel costs, and time off work, allowing patients to receive care from the comfort of their homes.
- Enhanced care coordination: Telemedicine facilitates collaboration between healthcare professionals, specialists, and patients, promoting continuity of care and efficient management of chronic conditions.

- Early intervention and improved outcomes: Remote monitoring and timely consultations can lead to earlier detection of health issues and intervention, potentially improving patient outcomes and reducing hospitalizations.
- Reduced healthcare costs: Telemedicine can decrease costs associated with travel, hospital stays, and administrative tasks, providing benefits for patients and healthcare systems alike.

Challenges of Telemedicine:

- Technology access and literacy: Unequal access to technology and digital literacy can create disparities in telemedicine access, especially for older adults and individuals in underserved communities.
- Data privacy and security: Cybersecurity concerns need to be addressed to ensure patient data privacy and security in telemedicine practices.
- Regulatory and reimbursement issues: Regulatory frameworks and reimbursement models for telemedicine services are still evolving, creating challenges for adoption and implementation.
- Limited physical examinations: Some medical conditions require physical examinations that cannot be adequately performed remotely.

Overall, telemedicine holds immense potential to revolutionize healthcare delivery, offering greater access, convenience, and cost-effectiveness. However, addressing the challenges mentioned above is crucial to ensure equitable access and ethical implementation of this transformative technology.

Dive into the Booming World of Wearables

The tiny world of wearables is packing a massive punch! These smart devices strapped to our wrists, clipped to our clothes, or nestled in our ears are opening up a treasure trove of opportunities across various industries. Let's delve into some exciting possibilities for entrepreneurs, tech-savvy minds, and even those with everyday ideas:

Healthcare:

- Imagine your smartwatch keeping an eye on your heart: It can track your pulse, oxygen levels, and even sleep patterns, alerting your doctor about potential issues before they even become symptoms. This remote monitoring can help manage chronic conditions like diabetes and heart disease proactively.
- Stress got you down? Your wristband knows: By monitoring things like sweat, skin temperature, and even your voice tone, wearables can detect stress levels and suggest calming exercises or connect you with mental health professionals remotely.
- Working out just got smarter: Imagine a fitness tracker that not only counts your steps but also analyzes your form, adjusts your workout based on your real-time performance, and even cheers you on! This personalized coaching can maximize your fitness goals and keep you motivated.

Consumer Electronics and Retail:

- Shopping that feels like magic: Picture walking into a store and suddenly seeing personalized coupons and recommendations pop up on your smartwatch based on your preferences and what you're browsing. Wearables can revolutionize shopping experiences, making them more relevant and convenient.

- Step into another world: Augmented reality glasses can overlay digital information onto your real-world view, showing you restaurant menus on buildings, directions on your windshield, or even bringing historical characters to life right before your eyes. Wearables can blur the lines between reality and digital worlds, creating immersive experiences.

- Your home at your fingertips: Imagine controlling your lights, adjusting the thermostat, or even locking your doors with a simple gesture or voice command from your smartwatch. Wearables can seamlessly integrate with smart home systems, making life at home more automated and convenient.

Enterprise and Productivity:

- Safety first, always: Construction workers wearing smart helmets can be alerted to nearby hazards, while factory workers with biometric bracelets can be monitored for fatigue, preventing accidents before they happen. Wearables can enhance workplace safety and wellbeing.

- Lost packages are a thing of the past: Imagine delivery drivers wearing wristbands that track their location and update customers in real-time, eliminating lost packages and frustrating wait times. Wearables can revolutionize logistics and streamline operations.

- Data tells the story: Businesses can gather anonymized data on employee movements, preferences, and even work patterns through wearables. This valuable information can inform product development, marketing strategies, and even optimize office layouts for better productivity.

- Training gets high-tech: Surgeons can wear AR glasses that overlay critical information onto their field of vision during operations, while firefighters can receive real-time updates on building temperature and hazards through their smartwatches. Wearables can enhance training, improve performance, and even save lives.

Of course, with great opportunities come challenges. Privacy concerns around data collection, limited battery life, and ensuring compatibility across different devices are all hurdles to overcome. But with continuous innovation and ethical considerations at the forefront, the world of wearables is ripe for exploration and disruption.

So, whether you're a tech wizard with a revolutionary idea or simply someone with a keen eye for opportunity, don't underestimate the power of these tiny devices. Dive into the world of wearables, and who knows, you might just unlock the next big thing!

How Emerging Tools are Empowering Growers

Gone are the days of relying solely on gut instinct and sweat to make a living in agriculture. The world of farming is witnessing a thrilling revolution, fueled by a wave of exciting technologies. From tiny sensors in your soil to robots planting seeds and AI predicting the weather, these innovations are empowering farmers like never before! Let's dive into some specific ways they can thrive in this new era:

Precision Farming: Like X-ray vision for your field:

- Imagine tiny weather stations scattered across your land, whispering secrets about moisture content, nutrient levels, and even pesky pest activity. Smart sensors gather this data in real-time, giving you a precise picture of your field's health.

- No more one-size-fits-all approach: Based on this intel, you can tell your equipment to apply fertilizer, water, or pest control exactly where it's needed, not a drop wasted. Think of it as treating your field like a complex machine, with each part getting the specific care it needs.
- Drones become your loyal scouts: Picture these buzzing helicopters equipped with powerful cameras, soaring over your fields and capturing detailed aerial maps. These maps reveal hidden patterns, like areas struggling with disease or water stress, allowing you to take targeted action and save your precious crops.

Automation and Robotics: Your tireless farmhand robots:

- Picture tractors driving themselves, meticulously planting seeds or weeding between rows, tirelessly working even under the scorching sun. These autonomous robots take on the heavy lifting, freeing you up to focus on strategy and innovation.
- Livestock gets its own Fitbit: Imagine cows or pigs wearing fancy collars that track their health, mood, and even location. This data helps you detect illnesses early, optimize feeding schedules, and ensure your animals are happy and productive.
- Greenhouse farming on steroids: Think climate-controlled havens for your crops, where robots nurture them with just the right amount of light, water, and temperature. These high-tech greenhouses offer protection from weather extremes and boost yields year-round, even in harsh climates.

Predictive Analytics and AI: Your future-telling farmhand:

- Ever felt like the weatherman plays dice with your livelihood? AI-powered platforms, armed with vast amounts of data, can predict weather patterns, disease outbreaks, and even market fluctuations with surprising accuracy. This foresight helps you plan wisely, mitigate risks, and make informed decisions about your crops.
- Yields skyrocket with personalized advice: Imagine a digital farming assistant analyzing your data and suggesting the perfect planting times, fertilizer mixes, and irrigation schedules for maximum yield. It's like having a customized growth recipe for each corner of your field!
- Connecting directly with buyers, no middleman magic: AI can track market trends and connect you directly with potential buyers, cutting out the middleman and potentially fetching you a fairer price for your hard-earned harvest.

Challenges and Considerations:

- Tech-savvy farmers, unite! Learning to use these tools effectively requires training and support. Thankfully, numerous programs and resources are emerging to help farmers bridge the digital divide.
- Making tech affordable for all: The initial cost of some technologies can be a hurdle. But don't worry, innovative financing models and community collaborations are making them more accessible every day.
- Data privacy and security: As farms collect more data, protecting it becomes paramount. Robust cybersecurity measures and transparent data policies are essential for building trust and preventing misuse.

- Ethical farming in the tech age: We must ensure these tools are used for good, promoting sustainable practices, fair labor conditions, and responsible land management.

The future of farming is brimming with possibilities! By embracing emerging technologies responsibly and thoughtfully, farmers can become pioneers in a new era of sustainable, efficient, and profitable agriculture. So, are you ready to join the tech-powered farming revolution? The field awaits!

A Toolkit of Emerging Tech for Writers

The writing world is transforming alongside technology, and exciting tools are emerging to empower your pen (or keyboard)! Let's delve into some specific AI-powered helpers and innovative platforms that can supercharge your writing process:

AI Brainstorming Buddies:

- Jasper: Craft compelling content outlines, character descriptions, and even draft plots with Jasper's intuitive interface and powerful AI engine. Imagine outlining your entire novel in a flash!
- Rytr: Stuck on that first sentence? Rytr's AI can generate engaging opening lines, catchy headlines, and even blog post introductions, kicking your creativity into gear.
- ShortlyAI: Struggling with writer's block? ShortlyAI can analyze existing text and generate creative story extensions, unexpected plot twists, and even alternate endings, taking your story in uncharted directions.

Super-powered Research Librarians:

- Factcheck.org: Ensure your historical details and factual claims are airtight with Factcheck.org's comprehensive database and expert verification services. No more late-night Wikipedia rabbit holes!

- QuillBot: Need to paraphrase tricky text or condense lengthy research? QuillBot's AI helps you rewrite information while preserving your voice and key points, saving you precious time and effort.
- Copy AI: Researching marketing copy or crafting product descriptions? Copy AI generates persuasive ad copy, website blurbs, and even social media posts tailored to your target audience.

Eagle-eyed Proofreaders and Stylistic Guides:

- Grammarly: This classic tool catches typos, grammatical errors, and awkward phrasing, ensuring your writing shines with crisp clarity. Think of it as your ever-present editor, whispering suggestions as you write.
- ProWritingAid: Dive deeper with ProWritingAid's detailed analysis of overture words, clichés, and sentence structure. It helps you refine your style, boost readability, and elevate your prose to new heights.
- Hemingway Editor: Craft concise and impactful sentences with Hemingway Editor, which highlights overly complex phrases and suggests simpler alternatives. Perfect for writing with punch and clarity.

Virtual Acting Coaches and Character Whisperers:

- Character.AI: Need help bringing your characters to life? Character.AI lets you interact with AI-powered versions of your characters, developing their personalities, voices, and reactions through simulated conversations.
- Bard: It can assist with dialogue generation, exploring different character voices and personalities, and even crafting realistic conversations that propel your story forward. Think it as your collaborative co-writer!
- Murf: Give your characters distinct, expressive voices with

Murf's AI-powered text-to-speech technology. Create engaging audiobooks, narrated presentations, or even add vocal narration to your written work.

Beyond the Page: Immersive Storytelling Magic:

- CoSpaces: Craft interactive fiction experiences in 3D virtual environments with CoSpaces. Let your readers explore your world, solve puzzles, and make choices that shape the story.
- Talespin: Bring historical settings to life through VR experiences developed with Talespin. Imagine your readers walking the streets of ancient Rome or exploring the depths of the ocean alongside your characters.
- Simya: Engage your readers' senses with Simya's AI-powered tools that generate soundscapes, music, and even haptic feedback based on your text. Imagine readers feeling the rumble of thunder or the warmth of a campfire as they delve into your story.

Remember, these are just a few exciting examples! The world of AI and writing tools is constantly evolving. Be curious, explore new possibilities, and choose tools that align with your writing style and genre. And most importantly, never let technology overshadow the power of your own creativity and the human connection that drives storytelling.

Keep exploring, keep writing, and keep pushing the boundaries of what's possible! The future of storytelling is in your hands (and perhaps powered by a few amazing AI helpers).

Conclusion

Emerging technologies are reshaping the way we live, work, and interact with each other. While they offer immense opportunities and benefits, they also bring new challenges and risks that we need to address.

For example, AI and automation are transforming the labor market, creating new jobs but also displacing workers in certain industries. It is crucial that we invest in education and training to ensure that people have the skills and knowledge needed to thrive in a changing economy.

Similarly, gene editing and other biotechnologies have the potential to revolutionize healthcare, agriculture, and energy, but also raise ethical and social concerns that require careful consideration.

Moreover, the impacts of climate change are becoming increasingly visible and urgent, requiring immediate action to reduce greenhouse gas emissions, adapt to the changing environment, and build resilience in vulnerable communities.

Overall, the emergence of new technologies and the challenges of the 21st century demand a multidisciplinary and collaborative approach that involves stakeholders from different sectors and backgrounds, including scientists, policymakers, business leaders, civil society organizations, and the general public. Obviously, it provides a lot of business opportunities and money-earning potential without much competition, to the people who are interested in learning about them.

Thanks for reading this Book. This book aimed to provide an overview of opportunities available with emerging technologies, and the impact they may have on the future. I hope that the information shared in this book has given you insights into the potential of these technologies and the importance of staying informed about their advancements. Tell me your feedback about this book by sending email to rajamanickam.a@gmail.com

www.ingramcontent.com/pod-product-compliance
Lightning Source LLC
LaVergne TN
LVHW051331050326
832903LV00031B/3482

* 9 7 9 8 8 7 2 2 3 3 7 8 7 *